Using Critical Research for Educational and Social Change

This volume features the works of scholar-practitioners who embrace critical pedagogy and critical research as praxis in qualitative research about education. The authors take an explicit stance toward social justice through education, and they use critical research as a vehicle toward that end. The chapters critically engage with topics such as researcher role and position in critical research; collaborative research models with teachers and students; exploring visual epistemology in schools and with students; critical science education and cosmopolitanism; and developing praxis within teacher preparation courses and teacher research. Contributors push the boundaries of scholarship by presenting nuanced theoretical discussions or critical and timely educational issues via innovative forms of representation (i.e., fiction, narratives, dialogues, rich descriptions, and visuals).

This book was originally published as a special issue of the *International Journal of Qualitative Studies in Education*.

Dr. Tricia M. Kress is Assistant Professor at the University of Massachusetts, Boston, USA. She specializes in critical pedagogy, ethnography, and socio-cultural theory. Recent publications include *Critical Praxis Research: Breathing New Life into Research Methods for Teachers* (2011) and *Challenging Status Quo Retrenchment: New Directions in Critical Research* (2012). She is co-editor (with Robert Lake) of the book series, *Imagination and Praxis: Creativity and Criticality in Education and Educational Research*.

Using Critical Research for Educational and Social Change

Edited by
Tricia M. Kress

LONDON AND NEW YORK

First published 2013 by Routledge

2 Park Square, Milton Park, Abingdon, Oxfordshire OX14 4RN
711 Third Avenue, New York, NY 10017

Routledge is an imprint of the Taylor & Francis Group, an informa business

First issued in paperback 2018

Copyright © 2013 Taylor & Francis

This book is a reproduction of *International Journal of Qualitative Studies in Education*, volume 24, issue 3. The Publisher requests to those authors who may be citing this book to state, also, the bibliographical details of the special issue on which the book was based.

All rights reserved. No part of this book may be reprinted or reproduced or utilised in any form or by any electronic, mechanical, or other means, now known or hereafter invented, including photocopying and recording, or in any information storage or retrieval system, without permission in writing from the publishers.

Notice:
Product or corporate names may be trademarks or registered trademarks, and are used only for identification and explanation without intent to infringe.

British Library Cataloguing in Publication Data
A catalogue record for this book is available from the British Library

ISBN13: 978-0-415-83979-2 (hbk)
ISBN13: 978-1-138-37785-1 (pbk)

Typeset in Times New Roman
by Taylor & Francis Books

Publisher's Note
The publisher would like to make readers aware that the chapters in this book may be referred to as articles as they are identical to the articles published in the special issue. The publisher accepts responsibility for any inconsistencies that may have arisen in the course of preparing this volume for print.

Table of Contents

Citation Information vii
Notes on Contributors ix

Introduction: Inside the 'thick wrapper' of critical pedagogy and research
Tricia M. Kress 1

1. Stepping out of the academic brew: using critical research to break down hierarchies of knowledge production
Tricia M. Kress 7

2. Citizenship and social justice in urban science education
Christopher Emdin 25

3. Seeing what we mean: visual knowledge and critical epistemology
Carolyne Ali-Khan 43

4. Picturing oppression: seventh graders' photo essays on racism, classism, and sexism
Özlem Sensoy 63

5. 'Working with' as a methodological stance: collaborating with students in teaching, writing, and research
Christina A. Siry and Elizabeth Zawatski 83

6. Keeping a 'vigilant critique': unpacking critical praxis as teacher educators
Patricia Paugh and Elizabeth Robinson 103

7. Recovering from 'yo mama is so stupid': (en)gendering a critical paradigm on Black feminist theory and pedagogy
Rochelle Brock 119

Index 137

Citation Information

The chapters in this book were originally published in the *International Journal of Qualitative Studies in Education*, volume 24, issue 3 (May-June 2011). When citing this material, please use the original page numbering for each article, as follows:

Introduction
Inside the 'thick wrapper' of critical pedagogy and research
Tricia M. Kress
International Journal of Qualitative Studies in Education, volume 24, issue 3 (May-June 2011) pp. 261-266

Chapter 1
Stepping out of the academic brew: using critical research to break down hierarchies of knowledge production
Tricia M. Kress
International Journal of Qualitative Studies in Education, volume 24, issue 3 (May-June 2011) pp. 267-283

Chapter 2
Citizenship and social justice in urban science education
Christopher Emdin
International Journal of Qualitative Studies in Education, volume 24, issue 3 (May-June 2011) pp. 285-301

Chapter 3
Seeing what we mean: visual knowledge and critical epistemology
Carolyne Ali-Khan
International Journal of Qualitative Studies in Education, volume 24, issue 3 (May-June 2011) pp. 303-322

Chapter 4
Picturing oppression: seventh graders' photo essays on racism, classism, and sexism
Özlem Sensoy
International Journal of Qualitative Studies in Education, volume 24, issue 3 (May-June 2011) pp. 323-342

CITATION INFORMATION

Chapter 5
'Working with' as a methodological stance: collaborating with students in teaching, writing, and research
Christina A. Siry and Elizabeth Zawatski
International Journal of Qualitative Studies in Education, volume 24, issue 3 (May-June 2011) pp. 343-361

Chapter 6
Keeping a 'vigilant critique': unpacking critical praxis as teacher educators
Patricia Paugh and Elizabeth Robinson
International Journal of Qualitative Studies in Education, volume 24, issue 3 (May-June 2011) pp. 363-378

Chapter 7
Recovering from 'yo mama is so stupid': (en)gendering a critical paradigm on Black feminist theory and pedagogy
Rochelle Brock
International Journal of Qualitative Studies in Education, volume 24, issue 3 (May-June 2011) pp. 379-396

Notes on Contributors

Carolyne Ali-Khan is an Assistant Professor in the Foundations and Secondary Education Department at the University of North Florida, (UNF). Carolyne received her doctorate in Urban Education at the Graduate Center, CUNY in 2011. She is interested in investigating the ways that teachers and students learn about social others and in working with them to resist deficit narratives.

Rochelle Brock is an Associate Professor of Urban Education and Executive Director of the Urban Teacher Education Program at Indiana University Northwest in Gary, IN, USA. She is the author of the book *Sista Talk: The Personal and the Pedagogical* (2005) and co-editor of the books *Teaching Joe Kincheole* (2011), *Schools Suck: Arguments for Alternative Education* (2013) and *The Soul of Critical Pedagogy: The voices of People of Color in the movement* (2013). Her areas of research are urban education, teacher identity and Black feminist pedagogy. Rochelle is the series editor of *Black Studies and Critical Thinking* and the co-editor of *The International Journal of Critical Pedagogy*.

Christopher Emdin is an Assistant Professor of Science Education in the Department of Mathematics, Science and Technology at Teachers College, Columbia University, USA, where he also serves as Director of Secondary School Initiatives at the Urban Science Education Center. His research focuses on issues of race, class, and diversity in urban science classrooms, the use of new theoretical frameworks to transform urban education, and urban school reform. Recent publications include *Urban Science Education for the Hip-hop Generation*.

Tricia M. Kress is Assistant Professor at the University of Massachusetts, Boston, USA. She specializes in critical pedagogy, ethnography, and socio-cultural theory. Recent publications include *Critical Praxis Research: Breathing New Life into Research Methods for Teachers* (2011) and *Challenging Status Quo Retrenchment: New Directions in Critical Research* (2012). She is co-editor (with Robert Lake) of the book series, *Imagination and Praxis: Creativity and Criticality in Education and Educational Research*.

Patricia Paugh is an Associate Professor in the Curriculum & Instruction Department at the University of Massachusetts, Boston, USA. Her research interests include school–university research partnerships, equitable access to academic literacy for students in high poverty, linguistically and culturally diverse communities, critical literacy, and the value of practitioner research in teachers' professional development.

NOTES ON CONTRIBUTORS

She is the co-author of *A Classroom Teacher's Guide to Struggling Readers* and *A Classroom Teacher's Guide to Struggling Writers*. She has also published several articles and book chapters based on her collaborative research and teaching partnerships in urban public schools.

Elizabeth Robinson is a Doctoral Candidate in the Language, Literacy, and Culture Program at the University of Massachusetts, Amherst, USA. She also directs the teacher education program at Suffolk University in Boston, USA. Her research interests include critical literacy, critical pedagogy for English language learners, and investigating the meanings urban teachers make of educational research in their practices.

Özlem Sensoy is an Associate Professor in the Faculty of Education, an associate member of the Dept of Gender Sexuality and Women's Studies, and an affiliated faculty member with the Centre for the Comparative Study of Muslim Societies and Cultures at Simon Fraser University in Canada. She is the co-author (with Robin Di Angelo) of the book *Is Everyone Really Equal? An Introduction to Key Concepts in Social Justice Education* (2012).

Christina A. Siry is an Associate Professor at the University of Luxembourg, where she engages in inquiry into children's interactions as they learn science in multilingual classrooms. She is interested in collaborative inquiries and methodologies, and her research agenda focuses on elementary science education and elementary teacher education for science. Her work has been published in numerous journals including the *International Journal of Qualitative Studies in Education*, *Research in Science Education*, and *Science Education*, and she is a co-editor of the journal *Cultural Studies of Science Education*.

Elizabeth Zawatski currently teaches third grade in Darien, CT, USA. Previously she worked as a Special Education teacher. Elizabeth earned a Masters degree in Special Education and Literacy from Manhattanville College, USA. Her undergraduate degree, also from Manhattanville was in American Studies and Education. After working on various research projects where she reflected on herself as a learner, she became interested in students' motivations in school and is going to begin conducting research in this area.

INTRODUCTION

Inside the 'thick wrapper' of critical pedagogy and research

Tricia M. Kress

Department of Leadership in Education, Graduate College of Education, The University of Massachusetts Boston, Boston, MA 02125, USA

> This introduction provides a broad overview of the many 'whys' (existential, political, professional, and personal) for embracing critical pedagogy and critical research, which are reflected in this special issue as a whole. Scholar-practitioners of critical pedagogy and critical research hail from many disciplines and utilize various theories and methods, but all share the common goal of 'humanizing' education and research. Individually, the articles illustrate the many 'ways' and 'whys' of critical pedagogy and critical research. As a collection, the articles are representational of the power of the bricolage for the 'doing of' critical pedagogy and critical research.

Unwrapping the 'thick wrapper'

> Never does an event, a fact, a deed, a gesture of rage or love, a poem, a painting, a song, a book, have only one reason. In fact, a deed, a gesture, a poem, a painting, a song, a book are always wrapped in thick wrappers. They have been touched by manifold *whys*. (Freire 2006, 10, original emphasis)

There are many *whys* for embracing critical pedagogy and critical research, but the molten core of critical pedagogy as theory, as method, as *praxis* is a desire for and action toward a socially just world that is 'not yet' (Kincheloe 2008). It is a belief that the work of the critical pedagogue/researcher can help move the world a step closer toward a utopia that we may never witness but would mark the end of human suffering. Describing the purpose of critical pedagogy and critical research in this way is at once so simple, and yet so massive. Under this impossible mantra scholar-practitioners gravitate toward critical pedagogy and critical research for all sorts of reasons, and they practice their craft in many different ways. As a reflection of this, in the words of Paulo Freire (2006), this special issue is an event wrapped in a thick wrapper of existential, political, personal, and practical *whys* that call for scholar-practitioners to 'step out' of positivistic discourses and practices that limit the transformative and emancipatory potential of education and education research.

Existential, political critical pedagogy

On the macro level, critical pedagogy can be thought of as an existential quest and a political stance. Critical pedagogues seek to tap into the human potential while embarking upon a quest for the essence of humanity. They explore questions such as 'What are the epistemological, ontological, and axiological dimensions of being human?' 'How can we work toward creating a world that is more humane?' And 'What roles do education and research play in this quest for a more humane world?' Humanity here stands in opposition to the machine metaphors of global capitalism and progress (Giroux 1988), while rejecting the romanticized recapturing of a mythical 'ideal' humanity from some distant, provincial past. The humanity of critical pedagogy can be described as a dynamic process of being and becoming that is informed by present circumstances and historical context and is forward-looking into an unknowable future. It is humble, loving, and hopeful, and attainable through *conscientization* (a 'coming to awareness' of self and other in the world) and praxis (Freire 2007).

Underlying this existential search is the recognition that much of the world experiences pain at the hands of a minority who benefit from that pain. As such, the philosophy of critical pedagogy cannot be separated from the ethical dimensions and political implications of living in a world that is scarred by power struggles and inequality. However we choose to participate in this world, every human action and non-action has a political orientation and a moral consequence. Embracing critical pedagogy, as a form of action, involves making a commitment to fighting oppression that emerges from and maintains these power inequalities that negatively impact people's lives. Critical pedagogues/researchers recognize that oppression can be visible, taking the grotesque forms of genocide, enslavement, imprisonment, and exploitation, but it can also operate with a quiet violence under the cover of hegemonic discourses and imagery distributed via popular media and social institutions (like schools) (Kincheloe and Steinberg 2004). It is the belief of the critical pedagogue/researcher that as long as these forms of oppression and violence are allowed to continue, all of humanity will be prevented from reaching the existential ideal of humanness (Freire 2007).

Personal, practical critical pedagogy

Connecting this grand vision to the micro level of individual interactions necessitates a rethinking of 'what is' by questioning the commonsensical and seemingly benign daily rituals of life. In the world of education and education research, this means moving beyond 'instrumental rationality' by asking questions not just about the 'how to's' of education (i.e., how to teach, how to learn, and how to achieve on tests) but also about the *whys* of education (Giroux 1988). 'Why should teachers teach this content and in this manner?' 'Why should students be tested and ranked according to standardized measures?' Through critical questioning, critical pedagogues/researchers seek to reveal the ways in which macro social forces play out in micro-level interactions in order to expose the power implications behind these *whys* (Kincheloe 2008). They do this by asking, 'Whose values are represented (or not) in these practices and discourses?' 'Who is advantaged and disadvantaged?' And finally, 'What other possibilities are there for teaching, learning, researching, and living? How might we do or think about this differently?'

The resulting critical awareness of when, where, and how the socio-political and the personal intersect empowers critical pedagogues/researchers to purposefully enact their politics in their practice by pushing back against oppression and envisioning new ways of knowing and being. How this looks in action will vary greatly because critical pedagogy and critical research cannot be considered separately from socio-historical–political–economic contexts, the individuals who populate those contexts, and the scholar-practitioner's own relationship to these contexts and individuals. Furthermore, because power operates everywhere, the work of the critical pedagogue/researcher must be deployed on multiple fronts, from social policy to school policy, from preschool to professional school, from cultural studies to chemistry, from the individual to the collective. For this reason, critical pedagogy and critical research will have many different 'faces' as scholar-practitioner-bricoleurs utilize multiple theories and methods that are best suited for the task at hand (Kincheloe and Berry 2004).

A collectively forged bricolage

Inside this thick wrapper, the articles in this issue are simultaneously an echoing scream of frustration, a joyful celebration of solidarity, and a hopeful song of liberation. Together, they illustrate the diversity within critical pedagogy/research and the ability of critical pedagogues/researchers to operate on many fronts, while working toward the common goal of making education (and humanity) more humane. Common themes across the works are: dialogue, learning from difference, citizenship, collaboration, historical consciousness, alternative ways of knowing, humility, self-reflexivity, and social justice. Taken separately, the individual pieces describe research done in various locales (K-12 schools, universities, after school programs, the USA, and Canada) with diverse populations (middle school, high school, undergraduate, and graduate students from diverse ethnic and economic backgrounds) and with different theoretical and methodological approaches (critical literacy, Black feminism, visual epistemology, cosmopolitanism, co/auto/ethnography, critical discourse analysis, cogenerative dialogues). As a collection, they work together to form a bricolage of critical pedagogy/research that provides a complex vision of possibility for self, other, education, and social change.

'Stepping out' of the academic brew: using critical research to break down hierarchies of knowledge production

In the opening article, I theorize what it means to 'step out' of the academic brew by breaking down knowledge hierarchies and creating opportunities for dialogical learning and research. By utilizing a praxis framework of 'REDO' (reveal, examine, dismantle, open) I examine my interactions with the Young Researchers Club (YRC), a group of urban youth who design and conduct critical social research at an underperforming high school in Massachusetts. I reveal the ways in which the students have taught me how knowledge hierarchies are subconsciously maintained by more privileged adults (myself included). By revealing the ways in which the Young Researchers helped me to further develop self/other awareness, I illustrate the artificiality of the knowledge hierarchies that are created and enforced in academia, institutions of education, research relationships, and society more broadly.

Citizenship and social justice in urban science education

Christopher Emdin engages his readers in a discussion about urban science education as a matter of social justice and citizenship. The author illustrates the experiences of a group of urban high school students who reflected and perpetuated power inequalities in society within the classroom by limiting some students' access to learning resources and the classroom curriculum. By utilizing 'the three Cs' of cogenerative dialogues, coteaching, and cosmopolitanism, the author created a space where students (and teacher) recreated the classroom environment so that all students could participate in a process of 'citizenship' while learning about physics. The students and teacher discussed explicitly what democratic participation in a classroom might look like and how they could contribute to creating a more democratic learning environment. As a whole, the work has implications for education more broadly as we think about how we might utilize the classroom as a microcosm to promote a more democratic and socially just society.

Seeing what we mean: visual knowledge and critical epistemology

As explained and illustrated by Carolyne Ali-Khan, text-based messages are not the only ones that are being transmitted to students in schools, even as schools tend to limit learning activities to the written word. Students are also the recipients of many contradictory media messages embedded within visual images that can be found inside and outside school walls. In this piece, the author exposes the contradictory and often dangerous media messages that students encounter on a daily basis. She further implores her readers to work with students to interpret, critique, and create media messages so that students can push back against the educational industrial complex that positions them as consumers, while simultaneously representing them as innocent souls/criminal threats/underdog successes and misrepresenting the complexity of the world and the lives of urban youth who inhabit that world.

Picturing oppression: seventh graders' photo-essays on racism, classism, and sexism

In this piece, Özlem Sensoy shares with her readers one teacher's critical pedagogy in which a diverse group of Canadian middle schoolers learn to examine messages in visual media and use digital cameras to take pictures of and tell stories about their interpretations of racism, classism, and sexism. Sensoy's work illustrates the challenges of and potential for utilizing digital photography and digital storytelling in critical pedagogy. While some students created metaphorical and transgressive media narratives, most students interpreted oppression quite literally as discrimination based on skin color or hair texture. The metaphorical interpretations illuminate possibilities; however, the author also gives a note of caution: as illustrated by the more literal interpretations, the work of one critical pedagogue is hardly enough to incite transformational learning for all students. There is still much work to be done in helping students to think critically about how power operates in society.

'Working with' as a methodological stance: collaborating with students in teaching, writing, and research

Christina Siry and Elizabeth Zawatski discuss the power of coteaching, coresearching, cogenerating dialogue, and cowriting for developing teaching praxis and breaking down traditional classroom hierarchies in a field-based science methods course. The students and professors collaboratively designed and taught a curriculum unit together in an elementary classroom on a weekly basis during a semester long course. This approach challenged reductionistic approaches to teacher education by creating an environment where preservice students and their professor learned together through shared teaching experiences. The importance of 'co' for individual and collective learning and growth is underscored as the authors Siry (the professor) and Zawatski (a student) share their story through a polyvocal approach that utilizes coauthored text interspersed with single-authored text boxes.

Keeping a 'vigilant critique': unpacking critical praxis as teacher educators

In this piece, Patricia Paugh and Elizabeth Robinson use critical discourse analysis to challenge their own critical pedagogy in a *Practitioner Research* course in an in-district master's program for in-service urban teachers. As many students began resisting the course content and class, the authors discovered that espousing critical pedagogy does not mean that the learning environments one creates will necessarily be empowering for students. Their story urges critical educators to engage in 'vigilant critique' (i.e., constant reflection and examination) of their own practice to prevent critical classrooms from becoming spaces of domination and indoctrination. Furthermore, critical educators must ground the curriculum in activities that consider and honor the lived realities of the students in the classroom. In this case, this meant being cognizant of the very real pressures and circumstances of teachers who are working within school cultures that are heavy with accountability and high-stakes testing and then tailoring the classroom activities to be meaningful for the teachers in the class.

Recovering from 'Yo' mama is so stupid ...': (en)gendering a critical paradigm on Black feminist theory and pedagogy

By taking an experimental autobiographical/fictional approach informed by Black feminist theory, Rochelle Brock in dialogue with her historical guide *Oshun* (the African goddess of love) explores the historical roots and contemporary implications of the rhyming game called 'the dozens' (also known as 'mother-rhyming') in the lives of Black women. Her readers join her on a journey toward a pedagogy of wholeness as she traces the historical roots of 'the dozens' from preslavery in West Africa into the slave trade and plantation communities in the USA and, finally, into the present time where mother-rhyming continues in the form of misogynistic and homophobic jokes that maintain race, gender, and class domination. By unpacking the ideological messages embedded within and transmitted through 'the dozens', the author builds a foundation upon which she and her students can continue to critique and ultimately begin to transform social, political, and economic institutions that reproduce social inequality.

Notes on contributor

Tricia M. Kress is an assistant professor in the Leadership in Urban Schools doctoral program at the University of Massachusetts Boston. Her research involves exploring the potential of critical pedagogy and critical research for transformative learning and social change.

References

Freire, P. 2006. *Pedagogy of hope.* New York: Continuum.

Freire, P. 2007. *Pedagogy of the oppressed.* New York: Continuum.
Giroux, H. 1988. *Teachers as intellectuals: Toward a critical pedagogy of learning.* Westport, CT: Bergin & Garvey.
Kincheloe, J.L. 2008. *Knowledge and critical pedagogy: An introduction.* Dordrecht/London: Springer.
Kincheloe, J.L., and K. Berry. 2004. *Rigour and complexity in educational research: Conceptualizing the bricolage.* London: Open University Press.
Kincheloe, J.L., and S.R. Steinberg. 2004. *Kinderculture: The corporate construction of childhood.* Boulder, CO: Westview Press.

Stepping out of the academic brew: using critical research to break down hierarchies of knowledge production

Tricia M. Kress

Department of Leadership in Education, Graduate College of Education, The University of Massachusetts Boston, Boston, MA 02125, USA

> Critical theory and critical research are undeniably useful for revealing oppressive social structures and challenging the status quo in the realm of grand theory; yet, they are also useful for creating knowledge structures when academics deploy them on the ground. This article explores how critical theory and critical research can be used to critique hierarchies of knowledge in academia and society in order to create new opportunities for learning and researching dialogically, a process that the author calls, 'stepping out of the academic brew'. Using the concept of REDO (reveal, examine, dismantle, open) and an example of critical research done with and by urban high school students, the author offers a framework for how critical researchers (with the help of those with whom they work) might begin flattening hierarchical knowledge structures in education, in themselves, and in life.

The burden of knowledge

> The idea that it is not really about what you know is solidifying itself each passing day. So I am left with this choice *dumb it down or forever be wasted potential*. That might sound illogical since you're always told that knowledge is power but coming from where I'm from, knowledge is a burden. (Spock's research journal 2009, emphasis in original)

In the Spring of 2009, one of my doctoral advisees invited me to co-teach a group of 10th- and 11th-grade students enrolled in 'Social Activism', an elective course at Urban High School (UHS), a 'failing' school in Boston, Massachusetts. Many of the students in the class had been labeled 'underperforming' or disruptive, and many were truant from their other classes. Yet, most of those enrolled in this course faithfully showed up to first period to learn how to conduct critical research complete with theoretical frameworks derived from critical social theory. They learned about Bourdieu's (1991) theory of social capital, Sewell's (1992) structure/agency dialectic, and the individual/collective nature of identity as described by Roth and Tobin (2007). They applied these theories to their lived experiences at UHS while keeping reflective journals and engaging in class discussions.

At the time, Spock,[1] the author of the quote at the beginning of this article, was attending the 11th grade. By luck of the draw, she had been scheduled to take the Social Activism course. She was not there by choice. That day, she boldly told her teacher that everything they were learning about was 'bullshit because it won't change anything'. She was right, of course; simply naming sources of inequality would not change anything. Being able to theorize about social inequality is not the same as doing something about it. And besides, when she sat down in her second period class, this language she was learning was useless, detrimental even, because in another classroom using critical theory could be construed as being oppositional and disrespectful to the teacher.

When Spock shared with me the above quote from her journal, her words struck a nerve: 'dumb it down or forever be wasted potential'. This kind of thinking ran counter to my lived experiences as a PhD and a White middle class woman for whom knowledge was a valuable commodity, a means of getting ahead. 'Dumb-ing it down' in my world would surely lead to wasted potential; whereas, for Spock, 'dumb-ing it down' guarded her against becoming wasted potential. This contradiction cut through my common sense reality as I was forced to consider the plausibility of her words: where Spock is from, 'knowledge is a burden'.

Bringing critical theory to the ground

The application of critical theory is undeniably a useful starting point for troubling existing hegemonic notions of education. It exposes the baldness of meritocracy and the achievement ideology (MacLeod 2009). It illuminates that education is not the 'great equalizer', it is the 'great regulator' that ensures that power and wealth will remain concentrated (mostly) in the hands of those who already have it (Duncan-Andrade and Morrell 2008). And it reveals underlying struggles over epistemology by illustrating how throughout history, some people's knowledge 'counts' while others' is tossed into the epistemological trash heap of society (Kincheloe 2007). Policies that we see today regarding education and research, indeed policies we have seen throughout the history of the USA (Lagemann 2000), are derivative of certain people's beliefs about which and whose ways of knowing are considered legitimate and valid in our public institutions of education (Apple 2000).

These 'certified' ways of knowing, what Apple (2000) calls 'official knowledge', that regulate education and society neither include nor recognize the knowledges of students like Spock; rather, they most closely align with a White, Western, middle class, heterosexual, male view of the world which is presented as 'objective truth'. For an academic like me, 'official knowledge' can appear commonsensical because it aligns with my lived experiences; whereas, for an urban high school student like Spock, this knowledge becomes burdensome because she understands the painful reality that in order to graduate high school, she must play 'the game of school' in which she is passive and unknowing, an empty receptacle waiting to be filled with 'facts' gleaned from a (mythical) White, Western, middle class, heterosexual, male view of the world that runs counter to her lived reality.

In UHS, knowledge can indeed be a burden because, for the most part, Spock's lived experience does not count; only knowledge of the state curriculum counts. She must 'dumb it down' and parrot back what is expected of her in order to pass her classes and pass her tests or else she will be wasted potential. There is no mention in her classes about the social inequality that she knows exists because she has lived it, and the more Spock knows about how inequality is perpetuated in her life and the longer it is ignored as she goes through school, the harder it is for her to deal with the oppression that she experiences every day. She further explained the burden of knowledge in this way:

> What I was basically trying to say was that I feel like the more you know about how the system is set up against you, the harder it is for you to go through the motions and come here every day knowing that, like, you're not getting, you're not getting the benefits you should be getting ... I think that, sometimes I think that if I wasn't as intelligent as I am, which isn't a lot, then I would be happier in this environment, but uh, I'm really frustrated.

Spock is simultaneously compelled to comply with and struggle against being positioned at the bottom of the knowledge hierarchy of school and society in order to get her diploma and hopefully have the freedom to determine her own place in the world.

Her words also touch upon the double-edged nature of being and becoming a critical researcher: on the one hand, it is empowering to have command of a language that challenges oppressive norms; on the other, seeing the depth of social inequality, including one's own oppression and/or complicity in oppression, and recognizing the impossibility of changing society in one's lifetime is disheartening. Being critical of social inequality, whether one comes from my background or Spock's, does not amount to much if that criticality is not used to change our own or others' lived realities. For the critical theorist, there is a very real danger of slipping into nihilistic despair, thereby allowing the status quo to remain pristine while he/she becomes bitter and impotent, all the while maintaining his/her status as a knowledge authority and, in effect, becoming part of the oppressor group.

In this regard, Spock's assessment of the limitations of criticality for affecting change are accurately bleak; yet, I still have faith that when critical researchers actively work to use criticality in an applied manner not just for revealing and deconstructing inequality but also for constructing new possibilities in education, there is the potential to dismantle and transform these same knowledge hierarchies that limit Spock's agency. To do so, criticality must be deployed to external sources of oppression, but it also must be used to dislodge the oppressor within, that is, those parts of us that are comfortably steeping in a warm bath of ideology that normalizes social and epistemological inequality. This act, applying critical theories purposefully to break down (not just critique) knowledge hierarchies and create new ways of knowing and being, is what I call 'stepping out of the academic brew'. In the sections that follow, I myself will 'step out' by providing a discussion about the knowledge hierarchies Spock and I are referring to and what it means to me to 'step out' of them.

With help from Spock and The Young Researchers Club (YRC, a group of high school students I work with in my research), I will illustrate how I 'step out' in my own research by undergoing a process that I refer to as 'REDOing' (Reveal, Examine, Dismantle, Open): consciously working to unravel the knowledge hierarchies that are within me while simultaneously working to REDO the hierarchies that emanate from the social structures around me. By illustrating the sophistication of the work that Spock and the Young Researchers do and how working with them has challenged me to see education and research differently, I aim to open discussion about how we might lift the burden of knowledge by exposing the artificiality of the knowledge hierarchies we create and enforce in education, research, academia, and society. From there, we may begin to envision education and research as collaborative processes that are ongoing, dialogical, reciprocal, and conscientizing for the teacher and student, and the researcher and the researched.

'Stepping out' of knowledge hierarchies, politically and personally

The knowledge hierarchies that Spock and I are referring to are intimately tied to Western ways of knowing and being and have their roots in colonialism and positivism. They permeate US society as a whole, but they are most obvious in institutions of education. In my own life as an academic, I feel these hierarchies acutely as I teach my classes and conduct my research. As Smith (1999, 56) explains, much of the knowledge that emerges from the academy has been developed by conducting 'research "through imperial eyes"'. This type of research takes: 'an approach which assumes that Western ideas about the most fundamental things are the only ideas possible to hold, certainly the only rational ideas, and the only ideas which can make sense of the world, of reality, of social life and of human beings' (Smith 1999, 56). Denzin, Lincoln, and Giardina (2006, 774) further explain that this type of Western academic research:

> [...] fails to recognize legitimate differences in 'ways of knowing' possessed by diverse groups and peoples, and imposes a Western sensibility and rationality on experience even when Western sensibilities and rationality are highly inappropriate and indeed meaningless.

This results in the colonization, domination, marginalization, and hierarchical structuring of knowers and knowledges.

In this mentality, any knowledge, approach to knowledge, or knowledge worker that does not align with the epistemological ideal of the rational Western man (often regarded as synonymous with 'science' or 'scientist') is relegated to a lesser positioning in academia and society because, supposedly, subscribing to this Western way of knowing places the inquirer on the path toward discovering objective 'truth' about the world. Accordingly, the White Western male way of knowing is ostensibly superior because it is divorced from sensations of the body that taint the mind's ability to reason; in contrast, women's and minorities' inability to bifurcate mind and body mark their ways of knowing as inferior and thereby incapable of discovering 'pure' knowledge (Kincheloe 2008b). When positioned in opposition to this 'ideal' epistemology, other ways of knowing are then defined as subjective, biased, emotional, political, irrational, non-empirical, impure, and flawed; in other words, they are defined as 'other' than and therefore *not* ideal.

For scholars such as myself who have been immersed in Western culture and Western notions of research and science, colonialism and positivism have been normalized to the point where they feel commonsensical and are often hidden from me even as I might embody and enact these norms. As Kincheloe and Tobin (2009, 513) point out, like Whiteness, 'many of the tenets of positivism are so embedded within Western culture, academia, and the world of education in particular that they are often invisible to researchers and those who consume their research.' Even if we identify as critical or postmodern, we will experience limitations in our abilities to critique this Western vision because of the ways it shapes our own ways of understanding the world. To an extent, we may be able to define what it is and how it operates in our lives, but without being introduced to other ways of knowing and without being able to see ourselves through the eyes of another, we might be hard-pressed to envision alternatives if this is the only world we know.

Kincheloe (2008b, 29) explains, 'As living parts of the world, we are trying to figure out the world from *within* the world. In such a situation we can only approach this task from existing cognitive structures that shape and obviously restrict our consciousness. We can only see what our mind allows', which is often what we are already accustomed to seeing. No matter how else we identify ourselves, we are also academics, which means we are part of the Western academic culture, even if we identify as being on the margins of that culture. Dialectically speaking, we complete the oppressor–oppressed relationship; our very presence at the margins defines and normalizes the dominant center, even as we struggle against that center. Lorde (1997, 380) paraphrasing Freire explains, 'the true focus of revolutionary change is never merely the oppressive situations that we seek to escape but that piece of the oppressor that is planted deep within each of us and only knows the oppressor's tactics, the oppressor's relationships'. Herein lies the moral imperative for those of us who identify as critical to consciously work toward 'stepping out' of the academic brew: we must continue to be vigilant in seeking out and challenging not only the outside oppressor, but also the inside oppressor who may guide our hands even as we struggle to resist his dominance.

'Stepping out', then, can be understood as both political and personal. Moreover, because everyone experiences the world differently depending upon his or her sociohistorical situatedness (Kincheloe 2008a), there are as many ways of 'stepping out' as there are creative and imaginative researchers. Whether they identify as critical researchers or not, many academics take this approach to research, even though they may refer to it by different names, such as 'activist research', 'engaged research', 'participatory research', 'indigenous research', 'feminist research', 'service learning', 'public intellectualism', and more. However we identify ourselves as researchers, 'the activities of research are human endeavors, reflecting the hopes, desires, and tensions of our social conditions' (Popkewitz 1984, 11). For me, 'stepping out' involves the purposeful creation of dialogical relationships that enable me to develop 'conscientization', or a heightened awareness of self, other, and the world (Freire 2007). Through dialogue (both face-to-face and text-based), I am able to critically confront my own ways of knowing and being as I engage with others who see the world quite differently than I do. This enables me to come to new understandings about myself, my practice, my students, my research participants, and the world around me.

'Stepping out' of the academic brew, at first, is an oppositional stance to academic knowledge hierarchies; however, it is not about simply turning my back on or walking out of the academy. In fact, it is quite the opposite. It involves making a commitment to always being and becoming critical; engaging in 'an evolving criticality that listens carefully to feminist, anti-racist, anti-colonial and indigenous voices' (Kincheloe 2008b, 27); and continually working within and against traditional academic knowledge structures. This means repeatedly sinking in, rising out of, rinsing off, and turning to gaze back upon the muddy academic waters from which I have arisen. In other words, 'stepping out' is a process, which involves having the resolve to say 'no' by refusing to collude in the colonization of minds and bodies (hooks 1994), including my own. This resolve is steeled by a desire for a different (perhaps utopian) future, in which people can contribute to the process of knowledge production and social change together as equals. Not only is this antithetical to the hierarchical design of education, research, and policy frameworks in which knowledge is transmitted from a more knowledgeable authority to an unknowing mass of bodies (Au 2010), it is tremendously difficult to imagine while immersed within the hegemony of US society where social hierarchies (knowledge-based or otherwise) are pervasive and considered 'normal'. Critical theory, then, serves as a filtration system that enables me to see through the ideological mud that slows or prevents social movement.

Furthermore, 'stepping out' also involves making a commitment to flattening knowledge hierarchies in my work and my life, which necessitates developing relationships with others around a shared common purpose while also holding a profound respect and appreciation for difference. 'Difference' as I refer to it here is not the 'difference' we hear about in leftist multicultural rhetoric, where it is 'thought of as tracing the boundaries of a sequence of experiences, cultures, and identities' (De Lissovoy 2007, 358), and beyond which the ideal society will be achieved by coming to see the fundamental 'sameness' of all people. On the contrary, in this work, difference is understood as socially constructed and embedded in relationships between and across people who populate various raced, classed, gendered, geographic, and temporal locations in the web of reality.

From this perspective, 'difference must not be merely tolerated, but seen as a fund of necessary polarities between which our creativity can spark like a dialectic' (Lorde 2003, 26). Difference can be used 'as a springboard for creative change within our lives' because as Lorde (1997, 375) further emphasizes:

> Somewhere, on the edge of consciousness, there is what I call a mythical norm, and within our hearts each one of us knows that we do not fit that norm. In America, this norm is usually defined as white, thin, male, young, heterosexual, Christian, and financially secure. Within this society, the trappings of power reside within this mythical norm. Those of us who stand outside that power often identify one way in which we are different, and we assume that to be the primary cause of all oppression, forgetting other distortions around difference, some of which we ourselves may be practicing.

It is through a process of humbling ourselves, listening for and engaging with difference and not distorting it into deviance, nor erasing it into sameness, that we will open up new possibilities for being in the world. We can then forge our own 'apparatuses of resistance and critique, methodologies and pedagogies of truth, ways of making real realities that envision and enact pedagogies of hope' (Denzin, Lincoln, and Giardina 2006, 777).

Breaking down knowledge hierarchies by REDOing

'REDOing' is the process that I go through (with the help of others) as I listen for, dialogue with, and learn from difference, while developing conscientization so that I may be better equipped to disrupt social and epistemological hierarchies in myself, my practice, and my life. It is important for me to stress here the significance of humility. REDOing cannot happen in isolation; therefore, the first step in REDOing is accepting just how much I don't know so that I may begin to learn about myself and the world alongside others. When I am humble, I am better able to reveal, examine, dismantle, and open as described below:

- *'Reveal' myself and the hierarchies within and around me.* Exposing who I am and my own historicity and ways of knowing will help me to understand how I perpetuate and resist knowledge hierarchies in my practice. Declaring and claiming my own standpoint is just one part of the equation. Many of the revelations I have had about myself and how I understand the world have occurred with the help of others who are dissimilar to me; revealing, then, also means making myself vulnerable to *being revealed* by others.

- *'Examine' myself and the hierarchies within and around me.* As I begin to see through other lenses, I reflect back on who I am as a person and an academic and how my location in the web of reality influences my ways of knowing and being. I think about the social structures that have formed me and how I have worked with or against these structures. I dialogue with others about their perspectives and mine, and I allow myself to also *be examined* by others. I raise questions about why I see the world as I do and consider how I might learn to see it differently.
- *'Dismantle' hierarchies within and without.* Being a successful academic means embodying hierarchies and participating in the cult of the academic, regardless of whether I desire this or not, so that I may interact successfully with others in my field and share my work in public forums. To do so, I must become fluent in this culture, which means that sometimes it is such a part of me that I don't even see it. Once I am able to recognize and understand how and where hierarchies are reproduced both within me and outside of me, I can work on pulling them apart, thereby allowing other voices and ways of knowing to permeate my own ways of knowing and the academy more broadly. As with the above two processes, dismantling hierarchies also means lowering my defenses and *allowing others to dismantle* my tendencies toward reproducing hierarchies as well.
- *'Open' myself and 'Open' up dialogue.* Opening works in tandem with the other three. Here, in the last phase of REDOing, I must allow the people and world around me to show me new possibilities for knowing and being. This doesn't mean allowing in only critical or marginal voices; I must also be open to dominant voices because there is much I can learn from anyone who holds a different view of the world. As I pointed out earlier, this is not about creating an exclusive 'critical club'. By creating spaces for authentic dialogue with those who have different life experiences, whatever they may be, I can begin to change the way I see and act within and upon my social world. This dialogue can be face-to-face or text-based, but it means enacting what Kincheloe calls 'radical listening' (in Tobin 2009). It involves having a patient ear, understanding others on their own terms, and, to the degree that this is possible, not allowing my interpretations of the world to lead me to pass judgment upon those whom I am in dialogue with.

To some degree, breaking down the process of REDOing into four separate parts is artificial. While there are certainly four (or more) processes that contribute to the breaking down of knowledge hierarchies, these are not exclusive from each other; rather, they are cyclical and overlapping. For instance, dismantling might occur by virtue of revealing and examining. Or revealing might occur through opening up dialogue. Rather than being a linear progression from one stage to another, I envision REDOing as a complex system (see Figure 1) in which all of these processes may be happening individually or simultaneously, and any of these may catalyze another.

As I engage in the process of REDOing, I begin transforming knowledge hierarchies, starting with those within myself, by stepping out of, back into, and again out of the academic brew. My goal is to alter the consistency of the academic knowledge 'solution' within and around me each time I wade back in. For this reason, once it has begun, REDOing can never be finished; I will always be 'in process'.

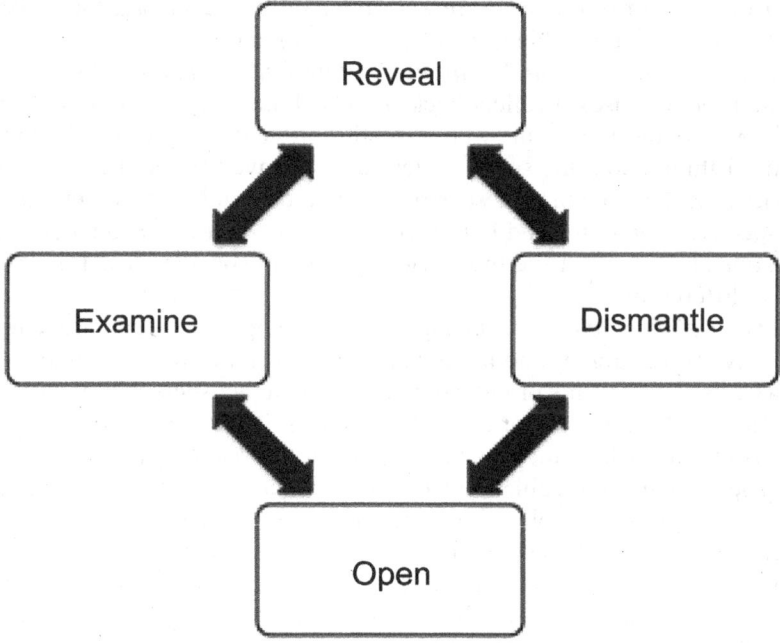

Figure 1. REDO.

In the following section, I will use my experiences with the Young Researchers of UHS to illustrate what REDO looks like in my life. I cannot claim that REDOing will occur in this same way in the lives of my readers; in fact, I would guess that REDOing happens differently for each person who engages in this process because it is personal and situated, and cannot be prescribed. However, by revealing how the Young Researchers have exposed me to new knowledge and made me more cognizant of my own taken-for-granted ways of knowing, I am able to show how we are in a symbiotic relationship, which creates opportunities for the development of new knowledge and culture in both the school and the university. This is quite different from more traditional researcher–researched relationships where the researcher enters the community, retrieves information, creates knowledge about the community in the academy, and then transmits that knowledge back to the community. While still, by virtue of presenting our story to an audience, I am the authoritative voice here, by positioning myself as subject alongside the Young Researchers, to a degree, I can disrupt the long-standing researcher–researched dichotomy. I can also illustrate the artificiality of academic hierarchies which historically have presupposed and preserved a unidirectional flow of knowledge from the university to the community, which 'excludes stakeholders from dialogue and active participation in the research process' (Denzin, Lincoln, and Giardina 2006, 774). In effect, by illustrating in this academic forum how the Young Researchers have helped to transform my ways of knowing and being, I am extending the process of REDO back into the academy.

REDOing with the help of the Young Researchers

To understand the significance of the work the Young Researchers and I have been doing, it is important to first know the context in which we work. UHS in Boston,

Massachusetts, typifies a US urban high school that is trapped in a seemingly impermeable and perpetual cycle of failure and reform. UHS is a Title I School. Most students are eligible for free or reduced lunch, which is a common marker of a high poverty school. More than two-thirds of the students are Black,[2] while the remainder of the students are mostly Latino, with less than 3% of the population identifying as White, Asian, or other. Twenty-five percent of the students have been categorized as special education, while 41.5% of students are eligible for Individual Student Success Plans (ISSP). The student mobility rate is 41.5%, the average daily attendance rate is 79.9%, and most striking perhaps, the four-year graduation rate is only 44.9%. Finally, in 2007, 78% of students did not pass either the English Language Arts or the Math MCAS (Massachusetts Comprehensive Assessment System) exam. As a result, in 2008, the school was not accredited, and at the end of the 2008–2009 school year, the school was restructured and merged with another 'failing' school.

In stark contrast to what this information indicates about this school, for the past two years UHS's debate team has dominated in the city of Boston, ranked near the top in the state, and ranked in the top 10 in the nation. The anomaly of the championship debate team representing the failing school is a beacon that illuminates what UHS students are capable of when provided with classroom structures that allow them to move beyond basic instruction that is often forced upon them for the sake of standardized exams. They can and do surpass their more advantaged peers when allowed to do so. The students of UHS are tremendously articulate, intelligent, curious, imaginative, and passionate about their education. The YRC, like the debate team, aims to capitalize on the students' talents and provide them with room and support to learn as intellectuals and not just exam-takers. The YRC emerged as a spin-off of the Social Activism course; students engage in critical social research, and they investigate questions that emerge out of their own interests, are drawn from their lived experiences, and are fueled by their imaginings of and desire for a more just society.

Even on the first day we met, the brilliance of these students was evident. For example, the research questions that the Young Researchers brainstormed very much resembled the questions that working academics and students at the university ask. The following is a list of just some of the questions that emerged from our first discussion:

(1) How does poverty affect education?
(2) What qualifies someone as a leader?
(3) How do aesthetics (i.e., physical appearance of the school facility) affect students' experiences with education?
(4) Where do stereotypes come from, and how do they impact people's lives?
(5) What is the role that parents play in inner-city students' education vs. suburban students' education?
(6) Why are impoverished people so exploitable/exploited?
(7) Why does the education system assume that parents can/will pay for a college education for their kids?
(8) Who really is responsible for failure – the individual or the system?
(9) Do people see themselves as victims of social reproduction?

Clearly, these are sophisticated sociological questions that university researchers continue to grapple with. The fifth question, for instance, is very similar to a research question one of my doctoral advisees is currently working on for her dissertation.

USING CRITICAL RESEARCH FOR EDUCATIONAL AND SOCIAL CHANGE

The following dialogue between me and several of the Young Researchers illustrates the sophistication of the students' knowledge of critical theory. In the excerpt below, the students and I are helping Scotty redesign his interview questions to help him to investigate whether people of different social classes and racial and ethnic groups recognize the social advantages and disadvantages that they have depending upon their positioning in society. He knew that asking people questions about this (especially if they come from privileged backgrounds) could be tricky and sensitive, so the other students and I helped him rephrase his questions so that they would be open-ended and exploratory, not inflammatory:

Scotty: I'll probably ask, 'Do you see yourself as the dominant class of society?'
TK: So that's, it's a good question, 'do you see yourself as the dominant class', but the minute you throw out the word 'dominant', most people are going to be like, 'I'm not dominant' because it sounds aggressive, right?
Scotty: Yeah.
TK: So how can we say that in a way that won't provoke that kind of reaction?
Kirk: Where do you see yourself in the social hierarchy?
Spock: (in unison with Kirk) ... social hierarchy.

While the other students assisted Scotty in diffusing the charged nature of his original question, Scotty recognized that the language they used might not be accessible to many people whom he wished to interview.

In the next exchange, they try again to rephrase his question so that it is more accessible to his interviewees:

Scotty: Now, if I was asking a group of students, 'where do you see yourself in the social hierarchy', how could I say that different because some people might not understand hierarchy? I want to phrase it more for, like, other people.
Zulu: Um, rankings of class?
Spock: How do you think you rank in society?
Scotty: Wouldn't that be like a dumb question?
TK: Well, even that's kind of strange ...
Scotty: That's like way, way dumbed down.
Spock: It is but ...
Zulu: Are you rich? Are you poor? Where do you stand in this little ...? (lifts up a square made of colored blocks)
Spock: Zulu, that's cute!
Zulu: (mutters) Shut up.
TK: So say the question again, and let's think about it.
Scotty: Um, where do you see yourself in the social hierarchy?
TK: Where do you see yourself in the social hierarchy? Umm...
Zulu: Where do you fit in ...

The students wrestled back and forth with the notion, and finally, Spock prompted the group to come up with an easier way to convey the term 'hierarchy', which, in the next exchange, led Kirk to develop a metaphor for thinking about Scotty's original question:

Spock: (interrupting Zulu) What's a simple word for hierarchy?
Zulu: ... in the structure of this ...?
Kirk: Pyramid.
Zulu: Yup.
Spock: If America was a pyramid, where would you see yourself?
TK: That's a great way to put it.

Zulu: But what if it's in the middle, and all these ...? (gestures hand, indicating hierarchical levels)
Kirk: Do you ... um ... do you see yourself at the top, middle, or bottom?
TK: That's a great way to put it, yeah. If America was a pyramid, would you see yourself at the top, middle, or the bottom?

In this short series of exchanges, the students illustrated that not only do they understand this theoretical concept, but their knowledge is sophisticated enough that they are able to translate it into a metaphor that nearly anyone can grasp.

Revealing

When I watched the video of the above exchange for the first time, I was tremendously humbled because I was analyzing this data for a talk I was giving in which I was going to show how the students engaged with complex theoretical ideas in order to illustrate the artificiality of the knowledge hierarchies we create and enforce in education. I had already created my *PowerPoint* slides for my conceptual frame, and on those slides, I used an image of a pyramid to illustrate what I meant by knowledge hierarchies. Yet, as I watched the video, I realized Kirk had come up with this same concept several weeks before I had; I just hadn't remembered it.

I am further humbled by my own feelings of awe, which I expressed at times while working with the students and while watching and reflecting on the video. This reaction *reveals* to me that the expectations I held for these students did not reflect what these students are actually capable of. Going into this project, my expectations of them were lower; although I didn't realize it. I was first made aware of this when Kirk said to me one afternoon, 'Don't look surprised, miss', after telling me he was on his way to the university to take a calculus course. My response was that I was impressed, not surprised, because his skill in math was much more advanced than mine was when I was his age. Yet, as I reflect on it, it is clear to me that there was also a part of me that was indeed surprised because of the very fact that he was more advanced than I was at his age; in fact, all of these students were.

Later in the semester, in a one-on-one conversation with Zulu, I explained that the work the Young Researchers do is very sophisticated, and people at the university are really impressed by it. His response to me was, 'I never thought of what we do as sophisticated. It just feels normal.' He was right, of course, that this activity is normal for these students; however, his comment *revealed to me* that it was not normal for me, other university academics, or the teachers and administrators in their school to regard this as normal for the students. Adults like me saw the Young Researchers' work as exceptional, while for the Young Researchers, this is just who they are and what they do.

Examining

After the students revealed my lowered expectations to me, I began to *examine* them and consider what they meant. While I believed the students were capable of more than what educators typically give high school students credit for, deep down, I did not see them as already capable of doing the same work that university students do. I was forced to question why that was so. Where did this lowering of expectations come from?

In the academic literature and in society, students in general, and urban students in particular, are often positioned as deficient. This stems from many things: our educational system is one that closely mirrors Freire's notion of 'banking', where students' minds are empty receptacles waiting to be filled with knowledge transmitted to them by more knowledgeable adults. This combined with numerous learning theories based on developmental readiness can result in expectations that limit the types of learning activities that students are exposed to in school. Urban students, especially those from poor and minority backgrounds, are seen as lacking because of racist and classist perceptions of these students, which are reinforced through underperformance on standardized exams that are (ostensibly) objective measures of students' academic abilities.

As a product of public schools, I experienced 'banking' and 'developmentally appropriate' education myself. School was never really about doing anything for real; it was always about 'learning to do' in order to be prepared to do things as an adult when you were in the 'real world'. Accordingly, I never felt I was treated as an intellectual in school until I was a doctoral student, and even then at times I was positioned as empty and 'in need of filling'. I recognized a similarity between the education I received and the education the Young Researchers received; yet, because of my knowledge of critical theory and the literature on urban education, I also saw these students as being at a greater disadvantage than I was because of our racial and economic differences.

As a critical pedagogue, I do not believe that education should be about banking information and always being at grade level; however, this is the only education I ever knew, so working against these ideologies is very difficult. I also do not believe that urban students from minority or underprivileged backgrounds are incapable of performing well as compared to peers who are White or economically privileged. Yet, sometimes, these preconceived notions, which are embedded in society, and to which I have been exposed in my own experiences and my academic training, surface in ways that I did not intend and are not immediately evident to me. My lowered expectations, while certainly higher than what these students typically encounter in their school, were still a product of White Western hegemonic notions of what it means to educate a child, specifically, an urban child from a minority or economically disadvantaged background. In some ways, my lowered expectations were not much different from those that Spock alluded to in the beginning of this article, when she said she felt she must 'dumb it down' in school.

Even though their teacher and I purposefully created this space so that the students would be treated as intellectuals, there was a deeper part of me that was surprised, not by what they were doing, but by the degree of sophistication with which they did it, because of my own social conditioning that kids are not as intellectually sophisticated as adults, and urban kids are even further disadvantaged when compared to their more privileged peers. Yet, my experiences of working with these students clearly negate this hegemonic logic. The research questions the students asked and the theoretical discussions they engaged in were on a par with (and sometimes more nuanced and developed than) the discussions I have with my doctoral students at the university. Although there are many problematic issues embedded in the assumptions I held, it is beyond the scope of this article to unpack them completely. In the interest of space, in the following section, I will dismantle just one of the major problem areas that I see: based on my preconceived notions, I assumed that these students needed a space in which to identify as intellectuals, and their teacher and I were able to provide that space for them. This indicates that I saw myself and their teacher as power holders and the students as powerless.

Dismantling

When this project began, I regarded the after-school club as a space where the students could identify as intellectuals, but the truth is, the Young Researchers do not need an after-school club to do that. In fact, they already identified as intellectuals, which is probably why they joined the club in the first place. The creation of the club simply made their intellectual identities more visible to me and others because through their association with this learning environment that *their teacher and I created, we identified them* and thereby certified them as intellectuals. This speaks more to the individual/collective nature of identity than it does to who these students are as individuals and what they are capable of academically. For example, on one of the videos, Spock explains this when she says, 'Even though I may not look that good on paper, I do things like this to prove to people that I'm not an idiot.' Spock is a championship debater; she has taught herself three AP subjects that are unavailable in her school; she maintains a blog in which she critiques social inequality; she borrows advanced sociological and theoretical texts from the public library (one day she was reading Foucault); she listens to music that has a political/activist edge to it; even her clothing expresses political statements. Spock already identifies herself as a critical theorist and an intellectual (although maybe not in those words), but others around her (especially adults) do not often see her on her own terms.

According to the school, Spock has a spotty attendance record; she challenges teachers and is sometimes defiant in class; she fails exams because she rejects much of what school tries to 'teach' her, which has resulted in a lower GPA than she is actually capable of achieving. By understanding Spock as a critical theorist and an intellectual, it makes sense that she doesn't perform to the best of her ability in a school where she feels she is treated 'like an idiot'; she rejects and resists structures (and people) that disrespect her and position her as deficient. In the hegemonic logic of education, Spock is not an A student because she is defiant, and she does not embody characteristics that are valued by the dominant culture (i.e., passivity, conformity, unquestioning acceptance of 'truths'). Until I got to know her better, I did not understand the extent to which Spock already identified as critical and intellectual. The YRC provided her and me with a structure to know each other, to dialogue together as equals, which enabled me to see her as agentic and not just a victim of an oppressive school system.

The YRC, like the debate team, provided Spock with another space (outside the confines of the classroom curriculum) in which to apply her agency in ways that were valued by the school. While I believe that providing students with this school-based opportunity to exhibit and develop their intellectual capabilities is valuable, in retrospect, I also realize that I was a bit pompous in assuming that their teacher and I knew and could provide what these kids 'needed' in order to identify as intellectuals. Students like Spock will create their own opportunities to cultivate their intellects with or without our help; we simply created an additional structure in which she could participate, one which also validated her intellectual activity as 'legitimate' in the eyes of the school and the university.

Opening

Once I understood the ways in which I simultaneously challenged and reproduced knowledge hierarchies in my practice, I began to listen more closely to the students and let them lead me to how they wanted to use this space, which often was just as time to dialogue about the world and their wonderings that emerged from their research and their lives. It became apparent to me over time that our discussions propelled deeper into the critical realm when the students led me, rather than if I tried to lead them, because they would apply the theory to their lived experiences. From session to session, I spoke less and the students spoke more, and even my physical location in the classroom changed. Unconsciously, I began sitting with them rather than standing or sitting in front of them. When they and their teacher requested it, I began sharing my data with them and dialoguing about the research I was doing. I had several lengthy one-on-one conversations with Spock regarding this piece that you are presently reading. She had a lot to teach me about knowledge hierarchies in society and how I (mis)understood them. For example, in the following quote, she challenged me to think about the ways in which kids already break down knowledge hierarchies:

> Maybe people are breaking down the hierarchies without knowing, like if a kid has a blog like online and, you know what I mean? Or like their *Facebook* statuses. And that becomes, like, if they have an idea, it's out there.

In the quote below, she challenged me to consider the ways in which academics position themselves as knowledge authorities by upholding previously established hierarchies:

> When you're trying to establish that you're an expert you usually quote other people, which, aren't you just establishing that they're experts, and that you just know what they said? ... So is there any other way to establish that you're an expert in something without using other people's work? ... Can't you just know?

Perhaps one of the most powerful moments of the year occurred when Spock, Kirk and Scotty came to watch a presentation I gave at the university. They sat around a large conference table with doctoral students, faculty, and the dean of my college, and during the question and answer portion, they dialogued directly with the academics in the room, all of whom knew a lot less about this topic than they did.

Bringing REDO back into the academy

> Honestly, the reality is that even if I'm like, I'm standing in front of you and I'm 'smart' in this environment, it doesn't mean – like I still don't know what I should know. Alright, perfect example, my SAT scores, I don't mean to sound conceited, but I got the highest in this school, but if you look at it on a national average, I suck ... I don't know what I should know and it's not necessarily my fault ... say I came in here, did what I had to do and got straight A's, right? If I went to an Ivy league school I would crash and burn because I don't know what I need to know, so I'm telling you, and even if I tried to teach myself, which I do, it's not enough. (Spock video transcript, spring 2010)

Kincheloe (2008b, 32) explains: 'thinking in new ways always necessitates personal transformation.' Such is the case as I engage in a process of REDOing, and I will not pretend this is an easy process. 'Change means growth, and growth can be painful'

(Lorde 1997, 380). In working with the Young Researchers and writing this article, I experienced many moments of pain as I realized the degree to which I unwittingly help to maintain hierarchies in education, but I believe the benefits of preventing the hurt I may inflict in the future are worth risking that initial pain I feel that comes from growing. As critical researchers take seriously the potential of critical theory enacted on the ground, I believe that by REDOing ourselves we can begin REDOing the world around us because in the end, we are individuals who together comprise the larger collective, and the world is what we make of it together.

By revealing the artificiality of the hierarchies I have helped to create and enforce, and by locating myself and my stance within academia, education, and society in general, I am better able to realize a vision of what I believe is the purpose of education. With the support of a like-minded collective, brilliant colleagues and young scholars who can help me to see my own epistemological limitations, I am able to push back against hierarchical knowledge structures by 'stepping out' rather than simply being pushed out or stepped on. I am better equipped to act on the beliefs that I hold about education and education research:

- I believe that knowledge is socially constructed, negotiated, and shared; it is not a collection of objects that is owned and exchanged like currency (Kincheloe 2005).
- I believe that intelligence belongs to all; it is not a gift bestowed only upon the privileged few (Malott 2010).
- I believe that education, at whatever level, can and should be more than what we allow it to be and, furthermore, it should not be damaging.

Being true to this stance in my work and my life involves making a commitment to 'stepping out' of (but not walking away from) the academic brew that suffocates so many minds, mine included.

My work with Spock and the Young Researchers has shown me that I am immersed in an academic embryonic fluid that has the tendency to anesthetize my imagination and prevent me from envisioning new possibilities in education (*reveal*). Pressures emanate from grades, standards, benchmarks, and reward systems (such as tenure and promotion) that feel comfortably normal as they depoliticize and justify the exclusion of those whose values and ways of knowing do not easily align with traditional academic values and 'certified' knowledges (*examine*). The domesticating ideological elixir of higher education is really not much different from the more aggressive epistemological policing that Spock is subject to in her high school (*examine*). I still find myself working hard to unravel deficit perspectives (mine and others'), even as I teach my doctoral courses (*dismantle*).

It is so easy to see what students do not know and what they cannot do, as opposed to what they do know and can do (*dismantle*). While I may know how to quote critical theorists, there is a whole lot more that, from their experiences, the Young Researchers know about urban education than I do (*dismantle*). As Spock pointed out, I can certify my knowledge with a quote or citation, but isn't it possible to also 'just know' (*open*)? Sometimes, my mind feels so heavy with academic culture that it seems like there is no world except the positivistic one that I am trapped in (*reveal*). Working with the Young Researchers has allowed me to see a glimpse of a different world outside my academic confine and the degree to which I actually help to create and maintain the world that confines me (*reveal, examine, dismantle, open*). The Young

Researchers have also enabled me to see possibilities (*open*). Maybe the academic bars between us are wider than I thought and we can walk through from one side to the other (*open*). Or, maybe, in the future we can work together to make sure those bars won't exist at all (*open*).

Acknowledgements
Thanks to Carolyne Ali-Kahn who coined the phrase 'stepping out of the academic brew' in a conversation with me as I was conceptualizing this special edition. Thanks to the Young Researchers, who have taught me more about knowledge hierarchies than academic texts ever could.

Notes
1. All names have been changed to preserve confidentiality. The students who participated in the Young Researchers Club, which appears later, actually selected their own names; they opted to use characters from the television show *Star Trek*.
2. Black is the racial category used by the city; however, the population of Black students is heterogeneous, consisting of various ethnic groups. Cape Verdean and Haitian are the two largest groups that comprise the Black population in the school, although there are others as well.

References
Apple, M. 2000. *Official knowledge: Democratic education in a conservative age*. New York: Routledge.
Au, W. 2010. The idiocy of policy: The anti-democratic curriculum of high-stakes testing. *Critical Education* 1, no. 1. http://m1.cust.educ.ubc.ca/journal/index.php/criticaled/issue/view/20.
Bourdieu, P. 1991. *Language and symbolic power*. Cambridge, MA: Harvard University Press.
De Lissovoy, N. 2007. Frantz Fanon and a materialist critical pedagogy. In *Critical pedagogy: Where are we now?* ed. P. McLaren and J.L. Kincheloe, 355–70. New York: Peter Lang.
Denzin, N.K., Y.S. Lincoln, and M.D. Giardina. 2006. Disciplining qualitative research. *International Journal of Qualitative Studies in Education* 19, no. 6: 769–82.
Duncan-Andrade, J., and E. Morrell. 2008. *The art of critical pedagogy: Possibilities for moving from theory to practice in urban schools*. New York: Peter Lang.
Freire, P. 2007. *Pedagogy of the oppressed*. New York: Continuum.
hooks, b. 1994. *Teaching to transgress: Education as the practice of freedom*. New York: Routledge.
Kincheloe, J.L. 2005. *Critical constructivism*. New York: Peter Lang.
Kincheloe, J.L. 2007. Critical pedagogy in the 21st century: Evolution for survival. In *Critical pedagogy: Where are we now?* ed. P. McLaren and J.L. Kincheloe, 9–42. New York: Peter Lang.
Kincheloe, J.L. 2008a. *Critical pedagogy*. New York: Peter Lang.
Kincheloe, J.L. 2008b. *Knowledge and critical pedagogy: An introduction*. Dordrecht: Springer.
Kincheloe, J.L., and K. Tobin. 2009. The much exaggerated death of positivism. *Cultural Studies of Science Education* 4, no. 3: 513–28.
Lagemann, E.C. 2000. *An elusive science: The troubling history of education research*. Chicago, IL: University of Chicago Press.

Lorde, A. 2003. The master's tools will never dismantle the master's house. In *Feminist postcolonial theory: A reader,* ed. R. Lewis and S. Mills, 25–8. New York: Routledge.

Lorde, A. 1997. Age, race, class, and sex: Women redefining difference. In *Dangerous liaisons: Gender, nation and postcolonial perspectives,* ed. A. McClintock, A. Mufti, and E. Shohat, 374–80. Minneapolis, MN: University of Minnesota Press.

MacLeod, J. 2009. *Ain't no makin' it: Leveled aspirations in a low income neighborhood.* 3rd ed. Boulder, CO: Westview Press.

Malott, C. 2010. *Policy and leadership in education: A critical pedagogy of educational leadership.* New York: Peter Lang.

Popkewitz, T.S. 1984. *Paradigm and ideology in educational research: The social functions of the intellectual.* London: RoutledgeFalmer.

Roth, W.-M., and K. Tobin. 2007. *Science, learning, identity: Sociocultural and cultural historical perspectives.* Rotterdam: Sense Publishers.

Sewell, W.H. 1992. A theory of structure: Duality, agency and transformation. *American Journal of Sociology* 98, no. 1: 1–29.

Smith, L.T. 1999. *Decolonizing methodologies: Research and indigenous peoples.* London: Zed Books.

Tobin, K. 2009. Tuning into others' voices: Radical listening, learning from difference, and escaping oppression. *Cultural Studies of Science Education* 4, no. 3: 505–11.

Citizenship and social justice in urban science education

Christopher Emdin

Department of Mathematics, Science and Technology, Teachers College, Columbia University, Box 210, 525 West 120th Street, New York, NY 10027, USA

> This article describes, and then applies a newly developed framework for classroom citizenship as an entry point into addressing social justice issues in urban science classrooms. The author provides in-depth descriptions of cogenerative dialogues, coteaching, and cosmopolitanism (3Cs), and presents this triad of tools as an approach to research/practice that addresses full participation of youth in an urban physics classroom. By describing the 3Cs, in an urban classroom, the author presents under-discussed issues that inhibit urban youth from fully participating in urban science classrooms, as an inhibitor to social justice within the classroom.

The chief premise that undergirds this work is that social injustice in the world outside of the classroom has a significant impact on what goes on within the classroom (Hacker 1995). Students absorb racial, ethnic, and gender-based stereotypes about their peers from different backgrounds, and bring these misconceptions into school with them (Nieto 2000). Once these stereotypes permeate the membranes of safe spaces like schools (which are supposed to be free from the biases that we encounter in the 'outside world'), they have deep socio-psychological effects on students (Williams 1999) and affect their abilities to engage in the classroom. Furthermore, if teachers and school personnel do not confront stereotypes that students have about each other, they promote a general disadvantage for students of color, who are most often the recipients of such bias (Hacker 1995; Kao and Thompson 2003). At a minimum, such unchecked bias, when encountered in the school environment, interferes with learning because students who are victimized by their peers may not cue in to classroom instruction. In most cases, they result in feelings of inferiority among certain students and inhibit their full participation in the educational process. I argue that the withholding of the power to fully participate from a student in the classroom is a form of social injustice that is just as significant as other forms of oppression that exist beyond the classroom.

While we traditionally think of social injustice as large enactments of unjust practices that oppress people or groups (Prilleltensky and Gonick 1996), I argue as Sue and his colleagues (2007) do that social justice is often perpetuated through microaggressions that seem delicate and are often overlooked, but have a tremendous impact on oneself. In classrooms, the enactments of social injustice are often subtle, and therefore, difficult to pinpoint. Therefore, maintaining or supporting social justice requires focusing on whether or not all students are engaged in the classroom. I argue that if students from diverse backgrounds are all fully participating, and empowered as scientists, a certain connection to each other and the classroom occurs, and a path towards social justice within the classroom is created.

The ability of a teacher to have *all* students (despite race, class, ethnicity, gender, or disability) be actively engaged in the class is the first step towards a socially just classroom, and indicates that the teacher is truly effective. Likewise, the ability of a society to support the participation of even the most marginalized people provides an indication of whether that society has the potential to move towards social justice. Therefore, I draw a comparison between the classroom and a nation as a means to viewing classroom practices as potentially influential to the smooth functioning of a micro-society that exists in the classroom.

Whether or not those in the margins are provided the space to converse, debate, reflect, and then have their needs met by those in power, or have the power to affect change indicates whether a society is democratic. Likewise, the ability of youth in classrooms to have their opinions expressed, their questions answered, and their reflections valued, indicates the extent to which the classroom supports the learning of *all* students (Hofstein and Lunetta 2004). Unfortunately, in society at large, the democratic values of participation and fairness that are indicators that social justice is valued are under-focused upon (Fung 2004). In other words, while we focus on democracy in society, or in a nation, it does not mean that all are participating or being treated fairly.

While participation and fairness are significant concepts to focus on in society at large, it is important to recognize that they are also important to focus on within classrooms. Classrooms are a microcosm of society, and the spaces where the injustices in the world beyond them are either replicated or reversed. Therefore, within classrooms, it is important to focus on subtle anti-democratic practices that reinforce stereotypes, do not consider all students, and force them to be individualistic, and understand that these types of practices are socially unjust. I argue that in the micro-society of the classroom, there can be a focus on participation and fairness and truly democratic spaces that meet the needs of all students can be created.

This is particularly the case in the physics classroom where: 'despite considerable evidence that traditional approaches are ineffective in teaching physics concepts, most physics students in this country continue to be taught in lectures and assessed individually' (Sokoloff and Thornton 1997, 342). In spaces like this, where lecturers dominate and assessment is purely based on written responses that are checked by the teacher without dialogue, opportunities to focus on participation and fairness (opportunities for all students to answer questions, share their challenges, or support each other) are rare. In these classrooms, solutions to problems are formula based and focused on an individual student's determination of an unknown quantity (Van Heuvelen 1991). Therefore, students do not get enough of an opportunity to pose their own questions, answer questions in class, or work with others to find solutions to them. This is particularly the case in urban classrooms, which, despite their goal to be democratic and include all students, are overwhelmingly focused on fostering autonomy (Lemke 2000). Autonomy in the classroom (whether it is implicitly or explicitly approved) undermines fairness, because it makes no accounts for the many differences in the classroom, and the fact that some students are more advantaged than others in regards to how they are favored by the curriculum (Altman 1970) and allowed to participate more than others.

In response to the issues surrounding how social injustice is inherited by, and the power differentials in, the science classroom, there are two main goals for this article. The first is to present a newly emerging framework for conducting research and engaging in pedagogy that focuses on citizenship and social justice in urban science classrooms. The second is to show how youth who have been disadvantaged by the structures of the urban science classroom have been allowed to have voice and move towards full participation in the classroom. To accomplish these goals, I use a triad of tools (3Cs) as a framework for research. These 3Cs are a piece of a more robust approach to urban science education that includes the 5 Cs of Reality Pedagogy (Emdin 2010). However, the 3Cs are focused on in this article because they serve as a means towards full participation through the concept of citizenship in the classroom.

I argue that in society, an individual or group with full citizenship has more opportunity to fully participate and be treated fairly. Each of the 3Cs addresses specific strands of citizenship, which when enacted, allows students to feel like they are fully participating, fairly treated parts of the classroom. I focus on citizenship in this work because when true citizenship is attained, there is a path towards equity and fairness. I argue that when individuals view each other as equally valued and respected citizens they have a common ground from which opportunities to support each other in learning can be fostered (Osler and Starkley 2003). Therefore, if urban youth view each other as citizens of the science classroom, they can move towards a socially just teaching and learning experience.

Theoretical framework

Citizenship

The overarching framework that is employed in this article is the concept of citizenship. I will first describe this process more broadly. And then, for the purpose of making sense of social injustice (the denial of full participation and fairness) in the urban science classroom, I will apply the concept to student experiences in classrooms.

The US Constitution describes citizenship as a process where privileges or immunities of *all* people who are considered citizens are undeniable (XIV Amendment, Section 1). Therefore, in its purest form, citizenship is a mechanism for addressing issues related to the full participation of and the provision of fairness for all people. However, as is the case when we describe the phrase 'all', as in 'science for all' or 'citizenship for all', realities of racial, ethnic, and linguistically diverse populations within the category of 'all' are often masked. Banks discusses this caveat of citizenship when he argues that if being a citizen revolves around just being within the nation and not being involved in the *social, political, and civil* processes within that nation, the process 'result[s] in the treatment of some groups as second-class citizens because [their] group rights are not recognized' (2008, 131) or exercised. In the urban classroom, this is a constant reality when only certain students are actively participating, and others, who often are new immigrants, seem to only serve as a backdrop to the dialogue being engaged in by the rest of the class. In these instances, all students are not enacting all three forms of citizenship (social, political, and civil).

As Lipman (2004) suggests, when there is a steady flow of immigrants into urban areas, an ever-evolving politics of race, class, and diversity is created where a new group is always available to be viewed as a partial participant in society. In urban classrooms, this dynamic is inherited and certain students are treated like partial participants.

In order to break the status quo, there must be a realization that full participation in the classroom and true citizenship are indelibly linked. Evidence of this full participation is attained when superficial involvement in the classroom and practices like responding to a question or raising one's hand to get the teacher's attention are not seen as the chief indicators of true participation (Kress, Jewitt, and Ogborn 2001). I argue that full participation/classroom citizenship involves all of the teaching and learning processes in the classroom, such as lesson planning, teaching lessons discussing the socio-emotional and physical dynamics of the classroom, and developing instructional approaches with the teacher. These practices align to the types of attributes that first class citizens would have within a society.

Banks (2008) discusses three strands of citizenship – *civil, political, and social* – that were first explicated by Marshall (1964) and help to further unpack the relationship between full participation and citizenship. These strands of citizenship are beneficial for addressing social injustice within urban science classrooms because they serve as a pathway towards equity for all citizens of a nation, and can become a model for what we look for in the classroom. However, it is important to recognize that in order to attain full citizenship, all three of the strands must be met. Bohman (1997) mentions that citizenship is most effective when it is not bestowed upon, or given. However, students are not perceived as able to advocate for themselves and not provided the tools to be more active citizens who can advocate for themselves (O'Donoghue, Kirschner, and McLaughlin 2002). Therefore, it is necessary to engage in a process that moves beyond the existent model of participation in the classroom where students cannot discuss their roles in the classroom, the students cannot teach and learn from each other, and the students have no set roles in the classroom other than to be passive participants that soak in information.

In many instances, the provision of one or two of the three strands of citizenship (civil, social, political) is perceived as sufficient for meeting the needs of the marginalized, and consequently, full citizenship is never fully attained. For example, the granting of civil citizenship to women through the call for women's right to vote, and the subsequent granting of political citizenship through the passing of the nineteenth amendment did not inhibit sexism or the social ostracization of outspoken women leaders because of the absence of social citizenship. Furthermore, attempts at social and civil citizenship for African-Americans in the late 1780s could never be achieved when political citizenship was denied by the three-fifths compromise. The point here is that inequities, without addressing the power structures that cause them, such as deep-seated bias, or the blind repetition of existent practice, develop into passivity in fighting oppression, which allows for people to be only partial citizens in society. Without a consideration for the three strands of citizenship, and the provision of an avenue to address these three strands in the classroom, neither full citizenship nor true participation can be attained. In the micro-society of the classroom, the three strands of citizenship are addressed through each of the 3Cs.

The 3Cs for urban science education

Individually, each of the 3Cs addresses a specific strand of citizenship (civil, political, and social). As a triad of tools, they enable educators to provide a set of collective steps that can give students opportunities for full participation in the classroom and consequently, provide opportunities for social justice (see Figure 1). While other work I have done focuses on 5 Cs by including content and context to cogenerative

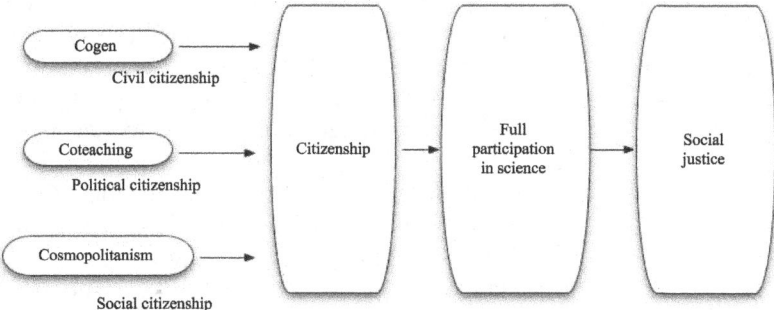

Figure 1. Diagram describing the 3Cs and their relationship to citizenship, full participation and social justice.

dialogues, coteaching, and cosmopolitanism (Emdin 2010), the 3Cs are the path towards citizenship, full participation, and eventually social justice.

The 3Cs have a significant purpose in the argument for social justice because they are not only tools for citizenship in the science classroom, but also essential tools for implementing what other researchers in social justice work have articulated as the goals of their work. For example, the five dimensions of multicultural education articulated by Cochran-Smith (2004) can be achieved through the 3Cs. These dimensions, which include using content from diverse groups in classroom instruction, helping students understand how knowledge is constructed, helping students develop positive inter-group attributes, helping them develop positive inter-group behaviors, and modifying teaching in ways that meet students' needs, are often articulated without the provision of a plan for implementing them. In the paragraphs that follow, I elaborate on each of the 3Cs and discuss how they can be implemented within urban science classrooms to achieve each of the specific strands of citizenship.

Cogenerative dialogues as a path towards civil citizenship

Cogenerative dialogues (cogens) are conversations with a group of students and their teacher about their experiences inside and outside of classrooms, with the goal of reaching collective decisions about the rules, roles, and responsibilities that govern their lives (Roth, Tobin, and Zimmerman 2002). Beginning with a few students and a teacher, and focusing on a science class that they all are a part of, teachers and students collectively decide upon at least one thing that the group can do to improve the science classroom. This strand of the 3Cs helps students to develop positive inter-group attributes and positive inter-group behaviors because they are connected in social spaces outside of the classroom where they can interact in ways that they do not have an opportunity to in the classroom. Cogens are a means to civil citizenship because the dialogues focus on having all participants in the dialogue be civil and respectful of one another.

Ideally, cogens occur with four to six participants who represent different groups in the classroom. The participants may be high and low achievers, students who both participate in the classroom and do not, or students from different ethnic or racial backgrounds. This structure allows for conversations to exist across groups of students that traditionally do not interact with each other because of the hierarchies that exist outside of and within the classroom. Because cogens ideally function with a small group that represents the different constituencies in the classroom, they are likely to be focused on specific issues that a student or group of students may have, and the creation of a possible solution to these issues. This process functions to create the space for urban students from various backgrounds to develop intergroup attitudes and behaviors that bridge existent cultural misalignments and misconceptions of each other.

Once consistent dialogues are in place, there are certain rules that are set in place so that they can run properly. The first is that all participants in the dialogues have equal turns at talk. All participants, including teachers, agree to not monopolize conversations. The second rule is that all participants within the dialogue engage in talk that is respectful of other participants. All participants are asked to listen attentively and allow their peers to complete their thoughts before responding. The third rule is that a plan of action for addressing issues raised in dialogues must be generated from the conversation and implemented in future classes. Throughout this process, students are able to become involved as researchers and practitioners in the teaching and learning of science in the classroom (LaVan and Beers 2005). They are also able to provide feedback to teachers about ways to improve instruction and able to see plans of action that they suggest in dialogues become implemented in the classroom. In this space, the biases that exhibit themselves both within and outside of the classroom are prevented from permeating through to the cogens because of a recreation of the norms of interaction and the absence of other peers who may cause marginalized youth to be oppressed in classrooms where they are the numerical minority.

Coteaching as a path towards political citizenship

Coteaching, another strand of the 3Cs, supports full participation in the science classroom by allowing the student to take on the role of teacher. Like cogens, coteaching supports positive intergroup attributes and helps students develop positive intergroup behaviors. Most importantly, it works towards modifying teaching in ways that meet students' needs by placing the student in front of the classroom and assisting them in communicating with peers from different backgrounds.

In traditional versions of coteaching, the perception is that interprofessional collaboration among teachers contributes to meeting the needs of children (Kenny, Sparks, and Jackson 2007). Coteaching, as used in this study, and when enacted alongside cogens, extends beyond this assertion by positioning students as the professionals in the distinct domains that affect their lives. Students become teachers – the ones who are responsible for their peers, and the ones who make the decisions about what is effective in the teaching and learning process. This take on coteaching varies from conventional forms where the professionals are teachers at different stages of their career (Roth, Tobin, and Zimmerman 2002) or from different disciplines such as content area and special education (Reinhiller 1996).

Coteaching provides students with opportunities to disclose their strengths and/or weaknesses in regards to the science content and share their general comfort or discomfort with particular topics. For example, in enacting coteaching, students can co-plan with the teacher, review the topic that will be taught in class, collectively decide on assignments, and then teach a lesson to their peers. These practices are designed to create opportunities for students to become active participants in the classroom. It also gives them the opportunities to both seek and exercise power in the affairs of the classroom, and actively work towards being more active participants. This process of seeking and exercising power that coteaching provides goes hand in hand with political citizenship because it is designed to allow a student to become more of an active participant in the inner workings of the classroom.

Coteaching aligns with political citizenship because it provides students with the opportunity to be a part of the inner-workings of the classrooms. Like political citizenship, which allows citizens to vote and become a part of the governance of the nation, coteaching allows them to make decisions about the chief goal of the science classroom and effectively deliver content. While political citizenship provides citizens with opportunities to be a part of the political processes that guide the society, coteaching allows them to be a part of the pedagogical process that guides instruction.

Cosmopolitanism as a path towards social citizenship

Cosmopolitanism is a philosophical understanding that focuses on the notion that all of humanity are citizens of the world and that each person has a responsibility for ensuring that all people are treated equally (Appiah 2006). In the science classroom, this philosophical understanding is translated into actual classroom practices that ensure that students enact social citizenship. While cogens more broadly focus on developing plans of action for improving the classroom, and coteaching involves the expansion of the role of the student to include that of teacher, cosmopolitanism is the focus on developing deep connections with students across racial, ethnic, linguistic, and gender differences by giving them responsibilities in the classroom that ensure that they move towards equity.

Cosmopolitanism in the science classroom requires giving roles to students that require them to enact practices that benefit others, and grading them for these practices just like they would be graded for a classroom assignment. For example, in a class where students usually do not get all the classroom materials that they should, assigning a role like distributor of classroom materials and grading students for ensuring that all students have all the materials, fosters a responsibility for others. Another way that cosmopolitanism is enacted in the classroom is through the buddy system. This process supports students who tutor their peers by giving them extra points on their classroom tests for taking the initiative to tutor another student.

Participants

This study was conducted in a ninth-grade physics classroom within an urban public school in a major northeastern city in the USA. Students in the science classroom were asked to be participants in the study and specific students who represented different demographics in the classroom were selected to be participants in cogens. In the school, 98% of the students qualify for free and/or reduced lunch and 99% of the students are classified as African-American or Hispanic. While the students in the classroom were classified as either African-American or Hispanic according to the school data, many of them classified themselves as having hyphenated American identities such as Dominican-American, Mexican-American, or Jamaican-American. This study focuses on a specific cogen group that had participants from the different ethnic groups in the classroom who were seated together within the classroom.

Methodological approach

Research design

This research was conducted as a means to investigate the effectiveness of the 3Cs on the attainment of social justice for students in an urban physics classroom. While social justice was the ultimate goal, the focus was full participation and developing citizenship in the classroom. The guiding research questions were:

(1) How does the 3C approach to citizenship address social justice issues in the classroom?
(2) Does/can citizenship, through the 3Cs, help students to be more empowered in science and more engaged in the classroom?

Data collection

Videotape Recordings (VTR), interviews, and field notes were the primary tools for gathering data. When VTR are combined with general observations and tools like semi-structured interviews, they are able to provide profound insight into what participants are thinking at certain points during dialogues (Grimshaw 1982). In this study, these data collection tools were helpful in identifying socially unjust practices in the classroom, when citizenship was denied to students, and when steps were taken towards addressing these issues.

While there were a few cogen groups with different compositions that engaged in dialogues, one group where each of the participants represented one of the ethnic groups in the classroom was the chief focus of the study. Once these students were in cogens together, the tenets of the dialogues were described by the teacher, and discussions about the teaching and learning in the classroom ensued. Cogens with this group occurred weekly for six weeks and conversations were mostly about what was working or not in the classroom. Students watched videotape of their classrooms, commented on parts of the video that indicated something out of the ordinary, discussed ways that the group could address these issues, and implemented their suggestions for improving the classroom.

When the cogen group that is the focus of this article studied videotape of their classroom, one of the chief things they uncovered was the fact that students were sitting in groups based on ethnicity. Furthermore, they were able to identify VTR where certain students were denied access to the teacher, books, or supplies based on their seats in the classroom. They were also able to identify how groups of students were denied opportunities to fully participate in the classroom. Over time, students were able to articulate the perspectives of their respective ethnic groups and how certain behaviors that they exhibited were either contributors to, or examples of the perpetuation of, social injustice in the classroom.

In early cogens, each of the students was encouraged to see themselves as a citizen of the science classroom (a fully participating student who treated others and was treated fairly). They were asked to talk about what it would be like to be a truly democratic classroom where all people's rights were preserved, all were treated fairly and respectfully, and everyone had an opportunity to teach and learn physics. Having students declare each other as collective citizens in cogens served as a tangible goal that they could work towards and a mantra they could follow over the course of the academic year.

In this study, coteaching was enacted through the invitation of students from cogens to join the teacher before school to plan science lessons. Students reviewed science concepts with the teacher, reviewed to each other, and then prepared for teaching the entire class. This process was designed to allow students to become more familiar with the physics concepts and go through the process of preparing for a lesson.

Cosmopolitanism was enacted by giving students from the cogen group roles that allowed them to be responsible for the rest of the class, such as tutoring their peers, preparing labs for the class, and cleaning lab stations. These students were then given additional classroom points/grades for enacting these practices. Over time, other students in the class were also allowed to take on these roles, and cogen groups were able to identify and demonstrate other ways that a student can be responsible for another's learning in the classroom such as being classroom artist (to draw diagrams for groups in classroom presentations) or a chart holder (who would hold another group's chart paper in front of the class).

While enacting the 3Cs, particular attention was paid to suggestions that emerged from dialogues that addressed instances where students did not, or could not fully participate. For example, if a student mentioned that a particular practice such as not getting a textbook caused her not to be involved in the classroom, the cogen group would ensure that the student and those who were in the same group would get a book during the next class. These practices, which were cosmopolitan acts, then became a set of practices that ensured that each student's needs were being met.

Data analysis

The data analysis process focused on detailed study of VTR from both cogens and classrooms. This video was analyzed in real time, slow motion, and frame-by-frame formats (Morse 1994) and interactions among students in each of these scenarios were closely studied. During this level of analysis, short VTR from the classroom were studied for patterns such as: which students were likely to come to the front of the class to answer questions, which students were generally more engaged, and which students were least likely to engage in the classroom. Following this step, there was an analysis/coding of cogens for points during the academic year that indicated when students were becoming aware of the need to view the classroom in a way that required viewing each other as citizens.

VTR from classrooms and cogens were then re-studied and the development of behaviors and practices prior to and after the implementation of the 3Cs was targeted. Here, there was a focus on students that initially did not speak to each other or their peers and students who were likely to inhibit their peers from participating and their behavioral shifts over time. In instances when students gained interest and participation, this progression was identified and the students involved were interviewed about what led to the change.

Lastly, I used classroom vignettes to generate questions for student interviews. Analysis of these interviews involved studying responses for information on what was going on in the classroom at specific points in time. For example, a group of students who began to answer more questions in class and form study groups with peers from different ethnic backgrounds were asked to respond to video from the beginning of the year when they were much less engaged in the classroom. These responses were then recorded and matched to students by ethnicity.

Findings

Challenging assumptions

The chief finding that illuminated other findings in this article was that students in the classroom would persistently group themselves based on affinity groups that were related to their race and ethnicity, but also their time in the neighborhood of the school. VTR of the classroom showed distinct ethnicity-based seating arrangements in the physics class. Puerto-Rican and African-American students sat at two different tables on one side of the room, and Dominican-American and Mexican-American students sat on the other side of the classroom. At the back of the classroom, there were three tables where Caribbean-American students sat and where other students that were of Latino decent but were not Dominican or Puerto Rican sat, and in the middle of the room, there was a mixed group of African-American and Puerto-Rican students (see Figure 2).

Another finding was that one of the ways that social injustice played out in the physics class was through clear and consistent practices related to the distribution of material resources in the classroom. In this classroom, like many urban high schools that serve students from lower socioeconomic groups, material resources such as text-books and lab equipment were limited. In these settings, where resources are low, the ways that students share the few materials they have provided insight into the assumptions they have about who has the right to materials, and what these assumptions mean for those who have access to science. The distribution of materials in the class supported certain students' full participation and ensured that others were not treated fairly.

For example, in instances when there were not enough books or lab materials for every student in the class, and not all students were able to have access to items that they needed to learn science, students who were not viewed as full citizens by their

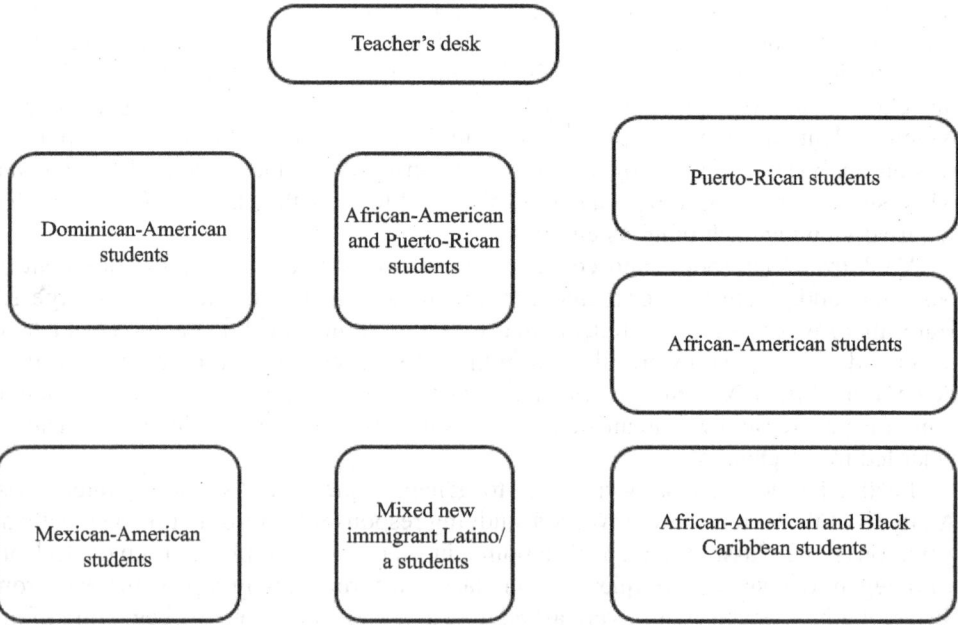

Figure 2. Diagram of the classroom layout and ethnic distribution.

peers did not have the same opportunities to use these materials as their peers. By keeping extra books/materials, certain groups of students ensured that their peers were repetitively deprived of science materials or books. For example, the class had only a set of 20 books for the close to 30 students in the classroom. However, when the textbooks were distributed, certain students who sat on the right side of the room would make sure that everyone in their groups would have a book while students from the Mexican-American or other than Puerto-Rican Latino/a group would not have any books for their entire group. This practice also happened with the distribution of materials for the creation of balloon-powered cars (during a lesson on speed and velocity) where students would have extra materials such as balloons or index cards but would not share them with students from certain groups who had little to no materials at all.

Students who were denied materials by their peers began to disengage in classroom activities. In some instances, VTR analysis showed students from the left side of the room attempting to make objections to being denied materials in the beginning of the year. However, as time went by, and their needs were not being met, they chose to disengage from the classroom. Over time, this process led to situations where the denial of classroom materials became a norm and students were directly affected not only academically but socio-emotionally. Jose, one of the students who was a new immigrant and newcomer to the school, raised this point in a cogen by saying, 'After a while, when I was just shut down and couldn't even talk in class, I started asking myself if I was really dumb or something.'

Another major finding was that the main victims of this form of social injustice were most often the Latino/a immigrant students. Not only were these students the recipients of limited resources, they were also subject to other classroom practices which limited their full participation, such as being interrupted when they spoke, being teased because of their accents, and having materials taken from them on a regular basis.

From the oppressed to the oppressor

Through studies of VTR and subsequent interviews with students from the classroom, I was able to identify certain characteristics that certain students had in common that positioned them as power wielders in the classroom that withheld opportunities for full participation from other students. For example, African-American and Puerto-Rican students, who were in the neighborhood of the school for the longest period of time, had similar accents, listened to the same music, and were a part of the same community organizations like after-school/community clubs, were primarily the ones who victimized their new immigrant peers. When they were with these peers, they would intentionally ostracize them by talking about shared experiences related to their time in the community that the new immigrant students did not know about.

For example, during one lesson, students who were from the middle table or the tables on the right side of the room would mention the Northeast blackout of 2003, neighborhood barbecues, and police chases that happened in the neighborhood. They continued these discussions even though their peers who had not experienced these events did not know what they were talking about. One student mentioned to a new immigrant peer that, 'You wouldn't understand what we are talking about … you were probably on a boat or something when that happened.'

The 3Cs as a means to providing citizenship and social justice

Once students who worked to exclude their peers and those who were excluded were engaged in the 3Cs together, particularly when they engaged in the planning phases of coteaching together, they reported in interviews that they spoke to each other outside of the classroom when they rarely did before. Furthermore, when confronted with video from the classroom that showed the ethnic and racial divisions and the ways that students treated each other, students were able to discuss their misconceptions of each other and the reasons for their behaviors.

Bonding through collective frustration

In this study, cogens and coteaching allowed frustration with the subject matter to be channeled into a necessary dimension of learning to participate fully. This frustration provided opportunities for students to expand on *the political and social* aspects of citizenship in the classroom. For example, in one lesson, different concepts and formulas related to work and force were explained to students. They all seemed to understand the lesson and were able to answer certain word problems related to calculating the net force acting on an object. In the lesson the next day, they were shown that there were more possible forces acting upon an object. They were then shown diagrams that depicted the types and directions of various forces that act upon an object. Students were then asked to draw an object, indicate force(s) that could be working upon the object, and calculate the work done by these forces. While they understood the lesson the first day, this lesson proved to be more challenging than the previous one. In a cogen group that was held right after this lesson during a lunch period, an African-American student named Erin commented that, 'This lesson made no sense ... How do you talk about formulas one day, and then all of a sudden start drawing diagrams?' A Puerto-Rican student named Linda mentioned that, 'He (the teacher) is combining too many things into one topic and this is frustrating.' A Dominican-American student named Carlos then responded by saying, 'I don't get this stuff either.' Janice, a Columbian-American student who rarely spoke in class said, 'Why are we drawing in physics anyway?' Erin then responded by saying, 'You're right, everybody agrees, this makes no sense.' These comments indicated that a number of students shared a level of frustration with learning about forces and work, and displayed the exhibition of civil citizenship among all participants.

This dialogue also led Jose, a previously silenced new member to the cogen group who was Mexican-American, to mention that he 'kind of understands the lesson'. Jose took out a piece of paper, drew a diagram, and explained a word problem that was a part of the previous lesson. Jose drew a free body diagram based on calculating the force of gravity acting on a 10-gram object, and then solved the problem based on the formula for finding the force of gravity with a given mass. He talked through the steps of the problem, and then looked up when he completed it. Erin asked, 'Is that the same problem?' and Jose responded by saying, 'Yes, it's just drawing the same thing.' Linda then drew a free body diagram question from the class earlier in the day, and said, 'What about this?' Jose then wrote out a word problem based on the diagram and solved it. Erin responded by saying, 'So that is the same problem', and proceeded to solve it on his own. He then said, 'This dude is really smart and is a good teacher.' As the rest of the group nodded in agreement, Linda said, 'Next time we have a test, I'm studying with you.' Jose smiled and Carlos agreed by saying, 'Yes, the other side of the class knows stuff too', and the students seemed to have overcome an obstacle together.

In an interview with Jose, three days after the cogen, and after his peers convinced him to teach the lesson to the entire class, he said, 'After coteaching was the first time I really felt like a part of the classroom. I loved when they asked me questions and I could just talk to them for once.' In another cogen, Erin, who previously prevented other non-African-American students from participating, was teaching an ethnically diverse group about Kepler's Law and said, 'I just want to do what I can to make sure that everyone understands the formula.' This quote indicated that the divides that existed within the classroom were slowly being overcome through the implementation of the 3Cs.

Through the research in this study, a well-known assumption that 'the repeated everyday experience of being treated as an inferior produces a public image of being an inferior' (Deutsch 2006, 18) was affirmed. However, it also became apparent that for groups who have been treated as inferior, the experience of being more central to classroom discussions can shatter these images of inferiority. In other words, once students who were previously victimized were able to teach their peers across ethnic groups, work with them in preparing lab materials, and display their knowledge of physics, students began to value each other's contributions to the classroom and the 'us' versus 'them' discourse that was previously present in the classroom began to shift. For example, about a week after Jose's initial breakthrough with his peers, Carlos and Linda volunteered to teach a classroom lesson on sound waves. As they taught, they were so clear in their explanations and purposeful in asking all students to be a part of the lesson, that they set a tone so that all students were accepted. Carlos asked a student from each table to solve a question and asked each group to assign a person the cosmopolitan role to come to the board to explain their solution, and Linda went to each group to help those who were struggling to understand the concept. I argue that selecting students to participate in cogens, empowering them by preparing them for coteaching, giving them the space to teach in the classroom, and then giving them general roles for the smooth functioning of the classroom supports their active participation and allows the classroom to move towards being a socially just space.

Changing the dynamics of full participation

As student opportunities to reflect on the social injustices in science class expanded, their participation in class appeared to shift in noticeable ways. For example, as time went by, students interrupted their peers from different ethnic backgrounds or who were newcomers to the community from speaking in the class fewer times than they had done in the beginning of the academic year. In addition, students began to work with each other across ethnic divides to work on classroom assignments. On one occasion, before a unit exam on work, energy, and power, students were captured on VTR quizzing each other across ethnic groups while their peers in the cafeteria remained in their ethnically separated groups.

Students' expression of citizenship

Once Carlos showed the class that he could solve a difficult physics problem, he created an environment where students who were also from the same ethnic group could be seen as more than just a group of people to pick on for being from a different cultural group. Once Carlos finally found a voice, he began being viewed as an academic equal and an expert on certain physics topics and, in the process, was able to shift the socially unjust practices that his classmates enacted into a value for what he brought to the classroom.

Another significant change that came as a result of this study was a shift in the attitude towards recent immigrant students that students who were the power wielders (who had been in the community the longest) had towards their peers. For example, Linda, the Puerto-Rican student who was part of the cogen group, was more willing to share her knowledge and empower peers from other groups as time went by. At some points during the school year, she would respond to a peer who answered a question by saying 'good job' or making other statements that affirmed that what those students shared had value. In addition, the more cogens she was engaged in, the more she would share the privileges she had, such as getting classroom materials and books, with peers from other groups.

Discussion

Despite the fact that the research that was conducted in this study falls under the umbrella of urban science education, it serves as a framework that is recommended for all classrooms where issues beyond the classroom affect the students' opportunities to learn within it. As the field of science education and other subject areas position issues that directly relate to the urban students' experience as secondary to other foci of the discipline like performing well on assessments, the ethnic divisions in urban classrooms threaten to hinder a large number of youth from reaching their academic potential and meeting these goals. In physics, which is a field of study that requires participation, group work, and peer instruction in order to be taught effectively (Redish, Steinberg, and Saul 1998), the absence of civility, fairness, and aiming for full participation threatens effective learning of the subject matter.

Adams, Bell, and Griffin (1997) discuss that teaching for social justice requires both a process and a goal. Full participation, which is a path towards social justice, has the 3Cs and citizenship as a process and goals to accomplish. Citizenship is what is held as an ideal (through the enactment of the 3Cs), and full participation, through its different strands, is what is consistently worked towards.

The 3C Citizenship Model provides a way to target socially unjust and oppressive practices and address these issues so students can connect themselves to the science classroom and feel like they are a part of science. By allowing a student like Carlos to teach a science lesson, even though he was formerly seated on what a student once described as the 'wrong side of the class', he is provided with the agency to fight misconceptions of himself and his ethnicity and create a space for himself and others like him in the classroom. Carlos, through the implementation of the 3Cs and its focus on citizenship, was provided with the opportunity to disrupt the power disparities that traditionally existed between recent immigrant students and the rest of the students in the classroom.

Social justice in science

Science has often been described as a patriarchal discipline (Harding 1993) and patriarchal spaces are those where 'oppression is enacted upon the least empowered members' (Valente 2001, 123). This is why the part of this study that focuses specifically on dialogues among students from different ethnic groups is so significant. Participation in the cogens, where no ethnic group is outnumbered, and everyone has equal voice, potentially redistributes the power dynamics in the classroom and allows the formerly powerless groups to find strength through their newfound positions as coteacher and citizen in the classroom. In essence, the study that is described in this article can be beneficial both in its outline of an approach to addressing classroom injustice and as an example of ways to practically enact approaches to addressing social injustice that is rooted in finding voice for marginalized youth in urban settings.

Conclusion

The uneven historical foundation to science, and the fact that students of color rarely see themselves as part of the discipline or the world beyond it, is itself a major issue in urban science education. However, within urban science classrooms, educators have the opportunity to position the classroom as a space where this replication of oppression through science is addressed. In so doing, students can be exposed to a new and more inclusive reality and can connect to science in profound ways. Therefore, urban science education has a major role to play in addressing social justice within their classrooms and/or creating possibilities for it beyond the classroom.

In the spirit of research such as the work of Basu and Barton (2007) that considers the funds of knowledge that urban youth bring to science classrooms or the work of Elmesky and Tobin (2005) that expands the roles of urban youth in the classroom, this work takes a step towards full citizenship and having democratic academic spaces for all youth.

References

Adams, M., L.A. Bell, and P. Griffin. 1997. *Teaching for diversity and social justice: A sourcebook.* New York: Routledge.

Altman, H. 1970. Teacher–student interaction in inner-city and advantaged classes using the Science Curriculum Improvement Study. *Classroom Interaction Newsletter* 6, no. 1: 5–16.

Appiah, K. 2006. *Cosmopolitanism: Ethics in a world of strangers.* New York: W.W. Norton.

Banks, J. 2008. Diversity, group identity, and citizenship education in a global age. *Educational Researcher* 37, no. 3: 129–39.

Basu, J.S., and A. Barton. 2007. Developing a sustained interest in science among urban minority youth. *Journal of Research in Science Teaching* 44, no. 3: 466–89.

Bohman, J. 1997. The public spheres of the world citizen. In *Perpetual peace: Essays on Kant's cosmopolitan ideal,* ed. J. Bohman and M. Lutz-Bachmann, 179–200. Cambridge, MA: MIT Press.

Cochran-Smith, M. 2004. *Walking the road: Race, diversity, and social justice in teacher education.* New York: Teachers College Press.

Deutsch, M. 2006. A framework for thinking about oppression and change. *Social Justice Research* 19, no. 1: 7–41.

Elmesky, R., and K. Tobin. 2005. Expanding our understandings of urban science education by expanding the roles of students as researchers. *Journal of Research in Science Teaching* 42, no. 7: 807–28.

Emdin, C. 2010. Reality pedagogy and urban science education: Toward a comprehensive understanding of the urban science classroom. In *Second international handbook of science education,* ed. B. Fraser, K. Tobin, and C. McRobbie, 67–80. New York: Springer.

Fung, A. 2004. *Empowered participation.* Princeton, NJ: Princeton University Press.

Grimshaw, A.D. 1982. Sound-image data records for research on social interaction. *Sociological Methods and Research* 11, no. 2: 121–44.

Hacker, A. 1995. *Two nations: Black and white, separate, hostile and unequal.* New York: Scribner.

Harding, S. 1993. *The 'racial' economy of science.* Indianapolis, IN: Indiana University Press.

Hofstein, A., and V.N. Lunetta. 2004. The laboratory in science education: Foundations for the twenty-first century. *Science Education* 88, no. 1: 28–54.

Kao, G., and J.S. Thompson. 2003. Racial and ethnic stratification in educational achievement and attainment. *Annual Review of Sociology* 29: 417–42.

Kenny, M.E., E. Sparks, and J. Jackson. 2007. Striving for social justice through interprofessional university-school collaboration. In *Advancing social justice through clinical practice,* ed. E. Aldarondo, 313–36. London: Routledge.

Kress, G., J. Jewitt, and J. Ogborn. 2001. *Multimodal teaching and learning: The rhetorics of the science classroom.* London/New York: Continuum International.

LaVan, S., and J. Beers. 2005. The role of cogenerative dialogue in learning to teach and transforming learning environments. In *Improving urban science education: New roles for teachers, students and researchers,* ed. K. Tobin, R. Elmesky, and G. Seiler, 147–64. New York: Rowman & Littlefield.

Lemke, J.L. 2000. Articulating communities: Sociocultural perspectives on science education. *Journal of Research in Science Teaching* 38, no. 3: 296–316.

Lipman, P. 2004. *High stakes education: Inequity, globalization and urban school reform.* New York: RoutledgeFalmer.

Marshall, T.H. 1964. *Class citizenship and social development: Essays of T.H. Marshall.* Westport, CT: Greenwood.

Morse, J.M. 1994. Designing funded qualitative research. In *Handbook of qualitative research,* ed. N.K. Denzin and Y.S. Lincoln, 220–35. Thousand Oaks, CA: Sage.

Nieto, S. 2000. *Affirming diversity: The sociopolitical context of multicultural education.* New York: Longman.

O'Donoghue, J., B. Kirschner, and M. McLaughlin. 2002. Introduction: Moving youth participation forward. *New Directions for Youth Development* 96: 5–7.

Osler, A., and H. Starkley. 2003. Learning for cosmopolitan citizenship: Theoretical debates and the realities of young adults. *Educational Review* 55, no. 3: 243–54.

Prilleltensky, I., and L. Gonick. 1996. Polities change, oppression remains: On the psychology and politics of oppression. *Political Psychology* 17, no. 1: 127–48.

Redish, E.F., R.N. Steinberg, and J.M. Saul. 1998. Student expectations in introductory physics. *American Journal of Physics* 66, no. 3: 212–24.

Reinhiller, N. 1996. Coteaching: New variations on a not-so-new practice. *Teacher Education and Special Education* 19, no. 1: 34–48.

Roth, W.M., K. Tobin, and A. Zimmerman. 2002. Coteaching/cogenerative dialoguing: Learning environments research as classroom praxis. *Learning Environments Research* 5, no. 1: 1–28.

Sokoloff, D.R., and R.K. Thornton. 1997. Using interactive lecture demonstrations to create an active learning environment. *Physics Teacher* 35, no. 6: 340–7.

Sue, D.W., C.M. Capodilupo, G.C. Torino, J.M. Bucceri, A.M.B. Holder, K.L. Nadal, and M. Esquilin. 2007. Racial microaggressions in everyday life. *American Psychologist* 62, no. 4: 271–86.

Valente, J. 2001. *Quare Joyce.* Ann Arbor, MI: University of Michigan Press.
Van Heuvelen, A. 1991. Learning to think like a physicist: A review of research based instructional strategies. *American Journal of Physics* 59, no. 10: 891–7.
Williams, D.R. 1999. Race, socioeconomic status, and health: The added effects of racism and discrimination. *Annals of the New York Academy of Sciences* 896: 173–88.

Seeing what we mean: visual knowledge and critical epistemology

Carolyne Ali-Khan

Urban Education, The Graduate Center, CUNY, 365 Fifth Avenue, New York, NY 10016-4309, USA

> As knowledge production, interpretation, and representation in educational settings rolls along Guttenberg's (text-based) track, the twenty-first-century world outside the doors of the schools and universities is exploding with visual ways of knowing and being. As visual text is silenced in education, it is simultaneously exploited in the marketplace. This article will examine some of the political, epistemological, and ontological questions that are raised by education's steadfast adherence to the reductionism of 'text only' in a richly multimodal/visual world. The author uses a short autoethnographic journey as a starting point to examine the connections between critical pedagogy and visual knowledge in the quest for an educational world that literally and figuratively sees more.

In the grand scheme of things

Life is elsewhere

My students are bored. They need to 'know' ancient Chinese history (for the looming New York State exams), and they can't find any reason to care. The T'ang dynasty isn't giving them any joy. I am unsettled by the idea that maybe they are bored because I am just an awful teacher, so I have been quietly peering into other classes. Over the past 18 years as an educator, I have seen lots (*thousands*) of bored kids. Or to be fair, kids that look suspiciously like they are bored. It is possible that I am an awful teacher, but my reach is not that of a superhero. I didn't bore them all.

Boredom is not the only problem. I have become increasingly aware of how terribly deep the mismatch can be between the school and the child. It hardly seems worth stating that it is with good cause that many kids don't much like school.[1] The urban teens I have worked with have expressed a myriad of reasons: there is the outdated curriculum, the endless rules, the sense of surveillance and mistrust, fragmented divisions of time (the school slop), the hard seats and the soft intellectuality, the cheery ('cheesy') posters, and dull self-important textbooks. While the classroom textbooks lie (often in every sense of the word) dutifully open, students, animated in a very different world, are often texting each other in emoticons under the table (Figure 1).[2] Classroom lessons may rumble along, but for many youth, as the Czech author Milan Kundera famously stated,[3] 'life is elsewhere'.

Figure 1.
Source: Purchased from http://www.gettyimages.com/ (Image #sb10069478n-001, Order #9726843).

Looking to see more
A peering backstage

What is going on? Answering this, critical pedagogues have problematized school life to expose structural inequities. The theorists of critical pedagogy, such as Joe Kincheloe (2001), Henry Giroux (2003), and bell hooks (1994), argue that the 'hidden curriculum' of school is a curriculum of power that reinforces current social hierarchical positions. Masquerading as meritocracy, it privileges those (individuals and schools) who have already benefited from the system, reifying their perspectives and lauding their 'strength', while simultaneously blaming or 'holding accountable' those who do not succeed. I have witnessed the way that this operates as a child, a teacher, and a researcher in schools, noticing how schools often succumb to the positivist logic of one way of being, one way of knowing, and a 'one right answer' world. This epistemological, ontological, and axiological narrowness comes at a great cost; I have seen countless students 'fail' out of schools that could not engage them and could not speak a language that mattered to them.

It is not easy to make school learning matter in a visually robust and information-saturated world. Keith Kenny (2009) argues that visual communication (or the use of the visual medium to exchange information) is on the rise in every area of life. Visual communication involves a powerful symbolic system that is different from (but no less competent and complex than) linguistic systems. According to Kenny, visual communication has become a major source of *our* knowledge (2009, 182, emphasis added). In the United States the visual has contributed increasingly to 'our' knowledge as a society, but I believe it has not been acknowledged (for the most part) as contributing to 'our' knowledge in *schools* (Figure 2). However, as I have noticed it, visual *rhetoric* (the art of using images to persuade) is alive and thriving in school spaces, both in its overt form (through the use of visuals in textbooks) and beneath the radar (as it is used by students and quite differently by corporations in schools).

Figure 2.
Source: Clipart.

Looking beyond inky fingers

Maria Sturken and Lisa Cartwright (2001) assert that *seeing* is arbitrary (we *see* all the time) – *looking*, in contrast, is directed. Gillian Rose refers to *visuality* as the cultural construction of sight (2007, 2). *Looking* (or *visuality*) is the act of making sense of what we notice in the world. In what follows, I examine images as pedagogy in schools. My intention is to encourage a closer *looking* at images in educational spaces, to problematize them and to raise questions for educators and researchers.[4] I first discuss visual images in schools that address the construction of childhood itself. I then turn to some of the other visuals that are prominent in school spaces, and in conclusion, I discuss some pedagogical and ideological considerations on the use (and abuse) of visual images in schools. The questions I ask include: How do images of children circulating in schools contribute to contesting notions about childhood? Aside from classroom lessons, what other visual knowledge is circulating in school spaces? How has the language of images entered schools? By whom is this visual knowledge created, with what messages, and for whose benefit? Why should visual methods be utilized more in classroom teaching to abet the creation of counter-stories and to resist hegemonic influences? I draw on insights from the disciplines of critical pedagogy, cultural studies, media studies and art theory, as I navigate the world of the visual in schools.

Halos, horns, and big wallets: the visual construction of childhood
Walking the halls with the ghosts of children past

What is a child anyway? Answering this question, psychologists, sociologists, educators, scientists, clinicians, and lawyers have raged across academe and popular culture, fighting to define the child. According to the case made by Anne Higonnet (1998), in addition to 'scientific' proofs (exorcized in text), *visual information* has also been instrumental to the cultural formation of current conceptions of childhood. While popular media is currently (and yet again) asserting that children are not what they used to be, and are (in contrast to the good old days) too old, too worldly, too sexual, too violent, too cognizant of things that should be beyond their ken (and therefore in need of more parental, educational, and policy control), Higonnet uses an analysis of art history to argue that the very notion of childhood innocence is itself suspect, and that it is largely a 'pictorial invention'. Using plates of paintings and photographs as accompaniments to her text, she illustrates how the Enlightenment created the idea/ideal of the innocent child, which was then reinforced and reified by an accompanying 'visual fiction' (1998, 8). Once a 'visual habit' (of accepting this pictorial truth) was in place, the advent of 'photography made it possible for the ideal of Romantic childhood to seem completely natural' (1998, 9). The pictorial provided visual evidence of 'children's true nature'. According to Higonnet, pictures tell a story of childhood, but the story has changed. Our current photographic discourse of childhood rests on a narrative that stands in opposition to the idea of 'childlike innocence' – the contemporary child is pictured as adult-like, overly knowing, and far from innocent.

As a society, we seem uncomfortable with the notion that children should know things that they are not necessarily taught in school, preferring the idea of their 'natural innocence'. In *The Way We Never Were*, Stephanie Coontz (2000) uses an analysis of history to argue that the demonization of youth today is supported by positioning them in contrast to the earlier, better times, yet in actuality, the 'Leave it to Beaver good ole' days' never were. She cites compelling social statistics to argue that the perfect world (and the innocent doe-eyed child) of the 1950s (for example) is a figment of our collective imagination, supported largely by the images on television. Kincheloe uses the movie *Home Alone* to shed light on the way that popular films support stories filled with 'adult hostility toward [postmodern] children' who both desire and *know too much* (2004, 235). In all of these cases, 'knowing versus innocent' children are anxiety-laden fictions, visual tropes that embody a good/bad binary and function to support adult fears about children.

Worldly kids: common images of children in print media available in schools

Ambivalence about children is also evident in the multiple and sometimes contrasting ways that children are visually represented through the images that are circulated in schools. Images of youth in schools can be found primarily on posters on the walls, the websites that advertise the schools and the print literature that is available to the students. In addition, 'school edition' (i.e., free) tabloid newspapers and national news magazines are widely available in schools. It is to these images that I now turn.

A few covers of *Time* magazine illustrate the ways that children have been photographed (and PhotoShopped) as knowing far too much for our comfort. Here are some examples: The 27 August 2007 cover features a white baby with a moustache and wild, long white hair. The text makes the claim that schools fail our smartest kids, but the picture shows a child who, in his adult–baby combination, is nothing short of monstrous (*Time* 2007a). The 27 March 2006 cover shows a white boy somewhere between the ages of 9 and 12 who is plugged-in to headphones and surrounded by orbiting electronic gadgets (cell phones, iPods, computers and wires) (*Time* 2007b). The blue screen he is staring at tinges his eyes, and his pupils are dilated to give him a vacant, expressionless, unfocused and dazed stare. The text reads, 'Are kids too wired for their own good?' The answer, according to the picture, is not up for debate. The child looks like a cyborg, half-human/half machine, and clearly someone to be both feared and rescued. The 3 November 2003 cover shows an 'ethnic' brown-skinned boy of about six or seven years of age reaching out of the magazine cover, to offer us a pill (*Time* 2003). His head is slightly tilted, he stares straight at us. 'You want it?' we almost hear him ask. The headline next to him reads, 'Are we giving kids too many drugs?' but the picture contradicts this, as we are not giving the child drugs but instead are being offered drugs by the child.

Echoing the theme of fear and suspicion of youth, the local New York tabloids, available for free in many schools, are constantly filled with images of poor black and brown kids who are portrayed as 'the problem' (Figure 3). Visually confirming the need for 'moral panic' over youth, they are often photographed in gang paraphernalia, suspected of criminality, involved in drugs or posturing defiantly into the camera. By and large, these images of urban youth support the observation of Eric Margolis and Sheila Fram who, citing Dorothy Roberts, note, 'The powerful western image of childhood innocence does not seem to benefit Black children. Black children are born guilty' (2007, 205). Meanwhile, to turn the page in the same newspapers is to find multiple full-page advertising that uses (mostly white) 'girls' (i.e., teenagers who are supposed to represent adult women) to sell shoes, make-up, clothing, and electronics. These model children (literally and figuratively) are the image of (airbrushed) perfection, their radiant smiles confirming their inherent goodness. In both the positive and the negative portrayals, the bodies of these children seem to be inscribed with a right-wing agenda: know 'the streets' and get rightfully punished, know consumerism and live happily ever after. Visual images provide the proof. Ironically, although they stand in opposition to each other, both of these tropes portray sophisticated beings:

Figure 3.
Source: Purchased from http://www.gettyimages.com/ (Image #57516697, Order #9726843).

one set of youth is worldly in the ways of crime, the other is savvy to the nuances of market hip.

'As you ought to be': images of schoolchildren

Perhaps it should come as no surprise that the images of youth as schoolchildren (both in the pictures used in schools and in those used to advertise schools) conform to a narrow theme that presents children 'as they should be', clean-cut obedient and innocent beings, perfect for what Freire (2005) called the banking system of education. Once again, the images carry ideological inscriptions if the students are middle class and/or white; by and large, we see them seated in an orderly fashion, presumably waiting to be filled with knowledge (Figure 4). If they are not, their bodies and behaviors tell us that they have all of the wrong knowledge and are in need of the school to save them. The most obvious example of this is the still relevant, (ridiculous) and hugely popular film 'Dangerous Minds' in which a tough, leather-clad Michelle Pfeiffer swept into a school to convince snarly urban youth to believe in education, in part by taming them with Butterfinger candy.

Regardless of which side children fall on, the images of youth that circulate in schools convey an adult ambivalence about what children know and should know. The dominant message appears to be that although we (as educators) may universally preach 'knowledge is power', we prefer children to know only the things that conform to adult ideas about them. These ideas do not benefit all children. According to the

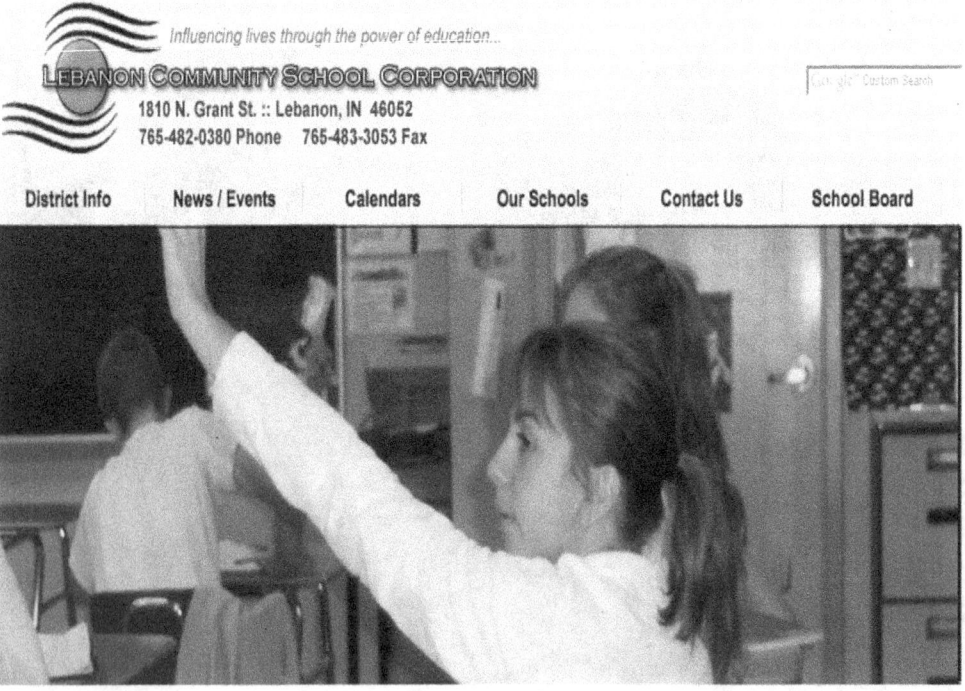

Figure 4.
Source: Screenshot. http://www.leb.k12.in.us/ (accessed May 3, 2010).

dominant visual narratives, children ought to be innocent beings waiting for knowledge to be bestowed upon them; if they are not, then they are clearly in need of the school to help remind them of what childhood should look like.

Images of children involved in school team-sports offer yet another definition of childhood. In contrast to the orderly contained child of the classroom, or the 'bad kid' of the tabloids, in the arena of school sports, sweating violence and bursting sexuality are not only allowed, but cheered on. In these images, the toughness of the jock is that of an adult, a woman/man who is able to withstand repeated physical pain for a good cause. The cheerleader is an almost entirely visual being. As a half-woman/half-child, she exemplifies the age compression that feminists (such as Kilbourne 1999) argue has become normalized in current popular and advertising culture. Straddling the space between child and adult, her visible-sexuality-in-the-name-of-the-team seems to allow her to escape the usual critiques about children and childhood. As a whole, I see the images of athletes in schools as providing for them a dubious space in which they are allowed to stand outside of the usual moral panic about childhood gone awry.

Ghosts in the machine: images of children that are **not** *seen in schools*

Monica Casper and Lisa Jean Moore ask us all to question how and why some bodies in contemporary society are hyper-exposed, while others are erased and denied (Casper and Moore 2009). The children (in particular the adolescents) who are *not* visible in the images of youth that surround us in schools, also speak of the way we are encouraged to think of children. There are many experiences and facets of the contemporary child that are often not evident in dominant images of them. The ways that youth have been betrayed and abandoned by adult institutions do not make it into popular visual discourses. Steinberg and Kincheloe (2004) point out that a postmodern childhood is one filled with adult stress, and it largely leaves children to fend for themselves in a world where mega corporations prey on their desires. Toby Miller (2009) notes that the perpetual *moral panic* about youth in the media, combined with the lack of *accurate representation*, renders youth paradoxically both the most silenced population and the noisiest. His point is that children, in particular teens, are overexposed through stereotypes they are supposed to embody, while simultaneously underrepresented in sympathetic portrayals of the complexity of their lives.

The children who are missing from the popular image are those who do not fit dominant narratives. I rarely see images of the many youth I have encountered in high schools, those who are not innocent, not dupes of the system, nor shallow and narcissistic (Figure 5). There is an absence of visual representations of the hard-working and responsible inner-city kids, who are not heroic in the celebrity tale of 'the star that makes it out of the "hood"', but who are heroic in the level of compassion, passion and laughter that they refuse to let go of and freely share, despite lives that are often grindingly brutal. Schools are not filled with promotional pictures of children who work hard to raise their siblings and tend to their elders, functioning as adults, as the social safety nets meant to hold their families have disappeared. The pictures of youth on the magazine racks in libraries aren't filled with the kids who quietly (legally or illegally, and often at great personal risk) do everything they can to provide economic support for themselves and their families as they seek to combat poverty in the 'land of plenty'. Inspirational posters in guidance offices don't show

'This image
is deliberately
left blank'

Figure 5.

the kids who have jobs and thus leave school every day to work long hours for as long as the jobs are there for them, and then search hard for new ones when they are not. Millions of young people: 'occupy a degraded borderland within the economic and cultural geography of neoliberal capitalism, in which the spectacle of commodification exists side-by-side with the imposing threat of the prison industrial complex' (Giroux 2003, xvi). I have had many hundreds of conversations with youth who are fully aware of the landscape Giroux speaks of, yet who summon the strength (that for all the times I have witnessed it I can still barely comprehend) to come to school, do the right thing and simply, with dignity, 'deal'. These children however are not the stuff of the images of children circulated in schools or in the media. They are ghosts in the visual machine.

Reloading the Matrix

I find these trends in the visual portrayals of children deeply troubling – in part because artistic, and in particular, photographic portrayals of children seem to have stood-in as placeholders for truth, framing the way we are encouraged to consider and interact with them. Özlem Sensoy elaborates on Richard Dyer's argument pointing out that 'how we treat others is based on how we see them; such seeing comes from representation' (2010, 43). Particularly with adolescents, the focus on what are often negative visual stories of them, highlights the popular notion of the pathology of youth and makes it difficult to place individual stories in a framework of structural critique. I argued at the start of this article that there is a mismatch between the child and the school, and I believe that popular images of youth circulating in schools contribute to this mismatch.

To literally *see* childhood as a construction is to begin the work of unraveling it. Analyzing images of children and images of schoolchildren can be a way for educators to thicken our reading of youth and begin to ask questions about childhood as a cultural construction. As images unveil their ideological inscriptions, we can look to other theorists for guidance in interpreting them. Michael Apple asks us to historicize current ways of talking about 'the problem of youth' (2001, xi). Nancy Lesko (2001) challenges common myths about adolescence, revealing them to be social constructions. Kincheloe urges us to problematize childhood as he cautions, 'Since childhood is a cultural construction shaped in the contemporary era by the forces of this media catalyzed techno-power, the need for parents, teachers, community members to study it is dramatic' (2009, 259). If we locate the construction of youth in the material practices of the visual medium (in particular photography and media), what patterns emerge? I have illuminated herein the patterns I see, and I ask, what do you see? As importantly, what do our students see? To approach these questions, we can ask students to make notes about the images they see of children and messages these images carry. We can ask ourselves if/how these images have influenced our own expectations of the students who come before us. As Kincheloe reminds us, 'We can reload the Matrix!' (Freireproject.org, n.d.).

She taught me to, walk this way: advertising images in schools

> Almost anywhere one finds children, their attempts to market to them, whether it's at doctor's offices or nature centers ... the jewel in the marketers' crown of commercial infiltration has been the nation's public schools. (Shor 2004, 85)

> Publicity adds up to a kind of philosophical system. It explains everything in its own terms. It interprets the world. (Berger 1972, 149)

Advertising has saturated the landscape of life, shaping the way we think (Kilbourne 1999), and it has also seeped into schools. Despite the outcry from organizations such as the Campaign for a Commercial-free Childhood, Commercial Alert, and the Media Education Foundation, as well as governmental initiatives such as 'Admongo' – an online advertising literacy game for tweens (Admongo.gov 2010), schools in the US at the start of the twenty-first century seem to make little attempt to stand outside of the matrix of corporate-driven commodity fetishism. Consumer Union (n.d.) has listed 234 companies that advertise in schools (consumerunion.org).[5] In support of corporate America's publicizing in schools, common arguments range from, 'it's harmless' and 'it's nice to help the kids' (by sponsorship that raises money for schools) on individual levels, to, 'we need to pay for our schools', as a typical administrative response. But if John Berger is right about publicity interpreting the world, then it is neither helpful nor harmless to have advertising in schools.

The high price of branding

Ironically, affirming the power of communicating through multiple intelligences and modalities, print advertising (which is the primary form of advertising in schools) speaks the multiple languages of text and image. Advertising and branding saturates children's worlds and this generation of children is deeply brand conscious (Linn 2005). A child who may have trouble reading a textbook can often read a Nike swoosh. As the visual pedagogy of materialism infiltrates childhood (and schools), it infuses into childhood the lessons of corporate capitalism. Marketers know this: currently companies spend over $17 billion a year on children's marketing, and children spend almost $200 billion annually (Campaign for a Commercial Free Childhood, n.d.). *Adweek* magazine recently published a special issue entitled *What Kids Want* in which they proudly, 'illustrate how companies are advancing their offerings to further get this young consumer demographic to pull harder on the family purse strings' (Adweek.com 2010). The cradle-to-grave branding of children teaches them (primarily through the use of visual images) powerful epistemological, axiological and ontological lessons: images are knowing, owning is being and being is achieved and crafted through materialism.

Peekaboo!: advertising images that are not hiding in schools

Encouraging kids to 'pull harder on the family purse strings' from the hallowed halls of learning, advertising images are infused through the school day. A few examples: Millions of students (who are required to cover their textbooks) receive free book covers and folders adorned with images of business products and services. P.T. Quigley (for example) has a revenue of $2.7 million (Zominfo.com n.d.) from supplying public and private schools with free school supplies on which they offer: 'The exclusive opportunity for a business or professional to promote their product or service' (P.T. Quigley.com n.d.). Walraven (a similar company) refer to themselves as 'a recognized and trusted name in in-school youth marketing'. On their website, they do not list their clients but simply show the images of logos[6] (http://www.walravenco.com/bookcovers/ourclients.asp). Most of the logos are immediately recognizable. Dairy Queen, Verizon, Dr Pepper, and the television station UPN43, nuzzle against each other on the screen in a bid for our interest. Words would clearly be superfluous. Classmates marketing (the name says it all) is a Walraven Company that distributes not only free book covers but also 'student reward coupons', with which to buy products from sponsored businesses. They supply advertising space on 'book covers, folders, bookmarks, pencils, rulers, erasers, classroom posters, notepads, mousepads …' The list goes on, and on, and on (Classmates marketing.com). The testimonials on their webpage gush with letters from schoolteachers, administrators, kids, and businesses. Randy Hester, the VP of Marketing and Communications at Cinemark, is an example. He writes, 'Our book cover program was a huge success. We had a 9% coupon redemption rate, letters from both kids and schools and an increase in hits to our web site' (Classmatesmarketing.com, Testimonials). Shifting to the spaces of physical education, Titus Sports Marketing 'can help you [the business] reach youth and parents at athletic events'. Their website logos, which are proudly displayed on the Titus site, include McDonalds, Capital One, Ford, Gatorade, Pizza Hut, the Marine Corp logo, etc. (http://www.titussportsmarketing.com/clients.html). Who needs words?

Advertising is not just on the print materials given to students. It is *everywhere* in schools. 'Reward coupons for students' are given to schools for local products (such as fast food). Teaching materials sponsored by corporations include logos and promos that are widely available to 'help' teachers. Educational posters in hallways advertise candy, footwear, movies, etc. Soft drink machines have logos and brand slogans. School lunch foods include brand symbols. Gyms, sports-fields, libraries, and playgrounds recognize donors by placing their logos in prominent positions. Educational websites are littered with advertising. School buses and school websites sell advertising space, and school lockers have also recently become advertising spaces (Figure 6). Free or low cost magazines (such as Sports Illustrated for Kids, Scholastic Choices magazine, and Scholastic Science World) are supplied to schools, carrying within them an impressive array of advertisers, including: Toys-R-Us, Hershey's, Pepsi, Maybelline, Reebok, US Air Force, and Clearasil (ConsumerUnion.com). Meanwhile, the infamous Channel One News provides schools with a free satellite cable system, TVs for classrooms, a cable network and more, in exchange for a teacher- and student-material–supported 12-minute news show with two

Figure 6.
Source: Campaign for a Commercial Free Childhood. 2010 (September 16). *A tale of two school districts*. http://commercialfreechildhood.blogspot.com/2010/09/tale-of-two-cities.html.

minutes of 'corporate sponsorships' (Channel One Help.com). According to the contract that Channel One schools must sign, the news must be shown for 90% of the days that the school is in session, and in its entirety, thereby *requiring* students to watch advertising.

Color me outta here!

While students are told to not run in the hallways, to read in turn, to sit in ordered rows, and to value reading over recess, images of advertising call on them to think of a very different life, and of themselves as very different beings in it. Kincheloe argues that the postmodern condition has 'torn apart meaning and affect' (1999, 7) and students 'quickly learn that school has nothing to do with their passions' (1999, 8). This fact has not been lost on advertisers who have worked to hijack the desire and passion of youth. The visual knowledge of advertisements in educational sites is snazzy, vibrant, and far from the 'boring' format of many classroom lessons. For example, one advertisement on a 'Channel One Assignment' page shows us a young buxom model in a white satin strapless dress. Her body is twisted as she thrusts her chest into the screen, her hands are on her hips, and her head is turned slightly to one side. She has flawless skin, 'perfect' exposed cleavage, a mane of tousled hair, pouty lips, and charcoaled eyes. The words next to her ask, 'or polished, SLEEK and sophisticated?' The logo under this simply proclaims, 'LG. Life is good.' LG is an electronics company that sells (among other things) washers, refrigerators, and phones (none of which are referenced in this advertisement). What makes life good here is not the products, it is the sexualized 'SLEEK', 'polished', 'sophisticated' model. She is a thing (like a refrigerator), and her valued 'sophistication' is that of a thing. Visual rhetoric that is aimed at youth offers them a distorted vision of an adulthood in which adults are nothing more than perfect, poised, and desirable objects. Color, movement, and often sexuality fill advertisement frames such as this one, which offer a window to another (more exciting) world, one that exists in sharp opposition to the humdrum architecture, pastel walls, and institutional visual aura of the school.

Mobilizing childhood desire, and/or youthful insecurities, advertisements aimed at youth (and circulating in schools) entice students to think of a place unlike school, a place where they are valued and in control. In this world, they are not just another kid in the system. Kincheloe notes, 'By drawing on the child's discomfort with middle-class protectionism and the accompanying attempt to "adjust" children to a positivist "developmentally appropriate" norm, advertisers hit on a marketing bonanza' (2009, 260). In particular, advertising to adolescents co-opts the subversive as it plays on framing them as major players at the center of a passionate, rebellious corporeal culture. This fantasy identity exists in a sub/cultural universe that is oppositional to the cerebral, dispassionate, adult middle class worldliness that is revered in schools. Pierre Bourdieu notes:

> The denial of lower, coarse, vulgar, venal, servile – in a word, natural – enjoyment, which constitutes the sacred sphere of culture, implies an affirmation of the superiority of those who can be satisfied with the sublimated, refined, disinterested, gratuitous, distinguished pleasures. (2009, 325)

As schools promote this 'superiority', the habitus of middle class, advertisers (in schools) capitalize on opposing it. As these ideological worlds collide, children are caught in the crossfire. This oppositional dynamic plays out in the broader framework of adult fear and moral panic about unruly youth. In addition, advertisers seem fully aware that unlike the success of good grades (which connects to the cultural competency of knowing how to play the game of school), the prizes of personal consumption are, at least in small increments and for a small fee, universally attainable. From a child's perspective, it matters that everyone can look 'slammin' in school, and the frowns of the adults just prove how much more kids know about the virtues of being hip. Battle lines are drawn. While schoolbooks tell them to see the beauty of poetry, the smiling faces on their Clearasil school book-covers show them that real beauty is skin deep. While we (as teachers) tell our students to value learning and being, the poster in the hallway tells them to value their shoes. In these 'texts', visual appeal takes the place of verbal reasoning, image stands in for truth, and logo recognition is honorable loyalty. As an example (proudly advertised on Channel One), *Dicks Sporting Goods* shows us an Adidas running shoe suspended over a young, athletically built African American male. He is muscular, his head is shaven, and his expensive sporting attire matches flawlessly. The camera catches him in motion. He is sprinting out of the frame, eyes intently fixed ahead. The words underneath him urge us in capital letters, 'SHOP NOW'. The messages in this image are additionally disturbing in their implication that for African American males, success is athletics, it is hyper masculinity, it is having an endless supply of new unblemished 'kicks' on your feet. It is also being ready to run. Fast.

Spectacle, capital, and the future

Douglas Kellner and Meenakshi Gigi Durham use Guy Debord to warn us, '"real life" is ... boring in this world, while the spectacle is exciting, enthralling ... (and) entangling its devotees in the clutches of consumer capitalism, replicating consumption fetishism, and helping capital to commodify all domains of social and everyday life' (2009a, 93). Using visual language and visual rhetoric, a vast network of consumer capitalism in schools offers young people tangible material successes that are bright and alluring (rather than ethereal and un-visible). Advertising is about an orientation to time and a promise of the future in which we see ourselves as better. The pictures and symbols of advertisements tempt students through a future that is more immediate than the distant 'better future' that educators make claim for. The future in which one owns new Adidas shoes is far more believable (both in its immediacy and in its scope) than the promise of 'education for happily ever after'. Many of the 'bored' students I have worked with have expressed being acutely aware of what it means to live in a crumbling economy where class mobility is largely a myth. As these students ask, 'why should I learn this?' in a world of bleak prospects, they are aided by visual stimuli that offer evidence for a world where visible success is possible, and sooner rather than later. Giroux notes, 'for many young people and adults today, the private sphere has become the only space in which to imagine any hope, pleasure, or possibility' (2003, xix). Although it is not an either/or situation, the cerebral joys of learning may be little match for the material gratifications that students can literally see in the school, just at their fingertips.

Seeing by the book: visual literacy in schools
Reading images

Visual literacy is not a priority in high schools, where images are usually treated as incidental. Margolis and Fram note, 'teachers largely regard the movement from pictures to words as one of intellectual progression' (2007, 55). In the lower grades, pictures are epistemologically validated as vehicles for communicating knowledge. (Young children are encouraged to communicate through images.) But as students progress through the grades, the (lack of) value given to images reflects the privileged position of text in the adult world. Whereas schooling for young children is multilogical (appealing to their affect and intellect) and multimodal (communicating through sound, text, and visual images), schooling for older students narrows to define factual text as the primary meaning-making tool and conveyer of knowledge.[7] Kincheloe (2001) argues that the 'facts' transmitted in school classrooms are usually less than factual but bursting with political ideology. Images in classroom teaching materials are also often thick with political ideological subtext. Wim Wenders argues, 'the most political decision you make is where you direct people's eyes' (Grosvenor 2007, 622). Images construct arguments that can operate beneath the radar of consciousness but send powerful messages. When photographs combine with text, they operate together as an authoritative discourse that makes an ideological claim to truth (Kenny 2009, 202–6). In order to teach our students to understand how pictorial truth-claims operate ideologically, we can learn from visual theorists and the visual rhetoric scholars who show us how pictorial images function as arguments (Olson, Finnegan, and Hope 2008). In what follows, I offer an example.[8]

Seeing others

Images in textbooks are influenced by the images in the broader socio-cultural and political context. This is particularly true with regard to how cultural 'others' are positioned. Dana Cloud points out that visual ideographs meld images and verbal (and often hegemonic) slogans to make abstractions concrete (2008, 394–5). Dominant narratives about 'others' enter the classroom through visuals that are not

Figure 7.
Source: Mayfield, C., and K.M. Quinn. 2007. *Mesopotamia*. Huntington Beach, CA: Teacher Created Materials Publishing.

unlike those found in public political spaces of TV, news magazines, the Internet, etc. 'By the time students "get to" studying the world ... they have already received a lifetime of media-based schooling about the world' (Sensoy 2010, 40). For example, currently, 'Muslims' are endlessly demonized as the 'new' enemy of the West. *Time* magazine has used photographs of Afghanistan to support an Orientalist positioning of 'Western reason' against 'Eastern irrationality' (Cloud 2008). Hollywood also has a long tradition of using negative images of those from the East to tell a demonizing story about them (Shaheen 2001; Steinberg 2004). Likewise, the visual images in educational materials about Muslim countries are frequently rife with political bias (Ali-Khan 2010) (Figure 7). Sensoy (2009) unpacks the images of 'The East' in school textbooks to reveal the divisive (and hegemonic) theme of ideological incompatibility between East and West. What these theorists are arguing is that commitment to democratic and anti-oppressive education involves commitment to closely examining images in classroom materials with an eye to the kind of reality they are aimed at constructing. It involves an awareness that 'language and systems of representation do not reflect an already existing reality so much as they organize, construct, and mediate our understanding of reality, emotion, and imagination' (Sturken and Cartwright 2001, 13). When we examine the ideological subtexts of images in educational materials, we gain a better understanding of both specific images and the claims they make, as well as the way that images work to position us as readers. As John Berger notes, 'we never look at just one thing; we are always looking at the relation between things and ourselves' (1972, 9).

Creating images as pedagogical practice

It's lunchtime and in my classroom a student is reading *Vibe* (a music and entertainment hip-hop) magazine. He studies the photograph of a celebrity, then launches into an argument with a classmate about the meaning of the image, all the while texting on his phone (at lightning speed) in a barrage of abbreviations and emoticons. His passion and ability to multitask are impressive, simultaneously communicating in words, abbreviations, and images. His skills are valued as cultural capital among his peers. Kenny notes that although there are several different types of communication systems available to us all, they are not considered equal; language systems are valued more than visual systems (2009, 46). Schools value one language system and students others – this prompts me to question the degree to which schools are equipping students to decode and read a world that is thick with visual knowledge (much of which is aimed at them). Are we able to equip them if we wanted to? In an increasingly electronically connected, multimedia, and visual world, my multimodal reach is far shorter than my students'. Are we engaging ourselves and our students in the quest to embrace this new multilogicality and to understand and communicate in an electronically based and increasingly ocular-centric world? Kellner and Durham argue for 'a postmodern pedagogy [that] is concerned to develop multiple literacies, to rethink literacy itself in relation to new technologies and cultural forms' (2009b, xxxvii). I concur.

Embracing postmodern pedagogy, Tricia Kress cautions, 'No educational initiatives, including technology initiatives, are free from value-laden historical and cultural resonances' (2009, 48); as educators we must also deal with 'the reality that we can never really be as postformal and democratic as we would like to be because we still have to navigate very real structures that, if ignored, could have very real consequences' (n.d., para. 31). With these warnings firmly in mind, there are still compelling reasons to embrace visual methods to create texts with our students. For one, we need the pedagogical ability to make complex ideas widely available to diverse audiences (Kincheloe 2007, 10). Without this ability, we not only bore our students but also do not speak the languages that they are versed in, and we do not equip them to better understand the workings of a rich multi-modal world. Roymieco Carter argues that when people are involved in creating and encoding images, 'the practice of critical inquiry becomes a sister conversation to discussions of form. Why use this image and not that image?' (2004, 295). The decisions made in creating visual text shed light on the production and construction of knowledge and truth. William Kealy (2004) points out that when students become producers of media, they become increasingly media literate, aware of the media in their lives and able to discern the politics inherent in the production of media (such as questions about who makes the choices in media images and for what purpose). To engage in visual knowledge production with students is to equip them to be both producers of images and critical consumers of them.

Even a passing glance at the pictures on cell phones or the *MySpace* pages of high school students confirms their engagement with the visual. Snapping pictures with their cell phones, even very young children seem perpetually prepared to freeze, posed for the camera, and to turn any moment into their celebrity moment. The extent to which they are influenced by media images with regard to their own construction of identity is a subject that merits careful consideration (but is beyond the scope of this paper). However, one way that we might learn how children navigate and interpret images is by tapping into their expertise. School-aged youth are already creating images and their skills may be far ahead of ours. Whereas those of us who did not come of age in the digital era may be easily overwhelmed by visual communication in hyperspace, our students' creativity and imagination in this world are fluid.

Such a move embraces a democratization of knowledge that is already (for better or worse) happening in the world outside of schools. Nicholas Mirzoeff notes that digital culture has 'empowered amateurism' (2008, 6). The 'publication' of pictures and photographs in cyberspace has led to a place where visual editorial decisions are no longer the domain of the select few. Arjun Appadurai points out, 'In the post-electronic world ... imagination has broken out of the special expressive space of art, myth, and ritual and has now become a part of the quotidian mental work of ordinary people' (2008, 175). The structures for the production of visual culture are in place (and in use in the private sphere of students' lives). Margolis and Fram argue that teachers need to be more sensitive to the range of resources that kids bring to classrooms (2007, 60). Christina Pedersen (2008) argues that images make ideas tangible, and because they can be multiply interpreted, they operate as a democratic space. Similarly, Donna DeGennaro and Tiffany Brown (2009) note how the power differential between teacher and student can be disrupted when students can become authors who create artifacts. Ideally, if we are able to build on the visual knowledge and creativity that students already use, we can learn with them, challenging what Freire (2005) called the banking system of education in which students are positioned as knowing nothing.

Spanners

Although I make the case for a greater use of visual methods in schools, I am aware that the path to this work is not easy. The institutional structures that Kress noted are formidable, and my experiences in trying to encourage students to venture into other communication languages (like hers) have been met with resistance. The habits of school are hard to break. In a world where students and teachers have been trained to jump through the hoops of standardized testing and to think in single right answers, the ambivalence of the images offers a serious challenge. Elizabeth Chaplin points out that images are 'polysemic, their meanings float' (2006, 43). This 'floating' intellectual space is substantially different from the one where 'what do I need to get an A?' exists. But if we do not embrace the challenge, then we reinforce the idea that only those who can 'do school' in the traditional ways belong, closing the door to those for whom the meanings of the world 'float'.

Closing thoughts on the meeting of visual and critical pedagogies
Looking forward

Critical pedagogy and visual studies are natural partners. Gillian Rose argues for a critical visual pedagogy as, 'we need to learn to interpret visual images because they are an important means through which social life happens' (2007, xiii). Kenneth Tobin notes that the visual field is a resource for the transformation and reproduction of culture, and that as we experience it differently (in schools), our experiences of school life differ (K. Tobin, pers. comm., 26 May 2010). To take seriously the visual image in schools is to examine the hidden curriculum both inside and outside the classroom, to step away from believing in a 'single right answer' world, and to take seriously the way that youth can be engaged or disengaged by the language systems used in school spaces. Kevin Tavin (2003) asserts that visual culture and critical pedagogy are dialogical partners as they both challenge disciplinary boundaries and problematize universal truths. My own experiences in classrooms confirm that the use of images can in part '(stem) the tide against the large numbers of disengaged students' (Flynt and Bronzo 2010, 528). By designating image literacy as important to education, we can work to illuminate the way that the power invested in images can work to privilege and validate some realities and to craft responses to this.

Although I have only touched the surface of the sea of images in schools, it has convinced me that more research needs to be done. The visual information that is circulating in school spaces is abundant and rich with meaning that both adults and children in schools are interpreting, but perhaps also dismissing. 'Schooling is only one site where education takes place. As a performative practice, pedagogy is at work in a variety of educational sites' (Giroux 2003, 38). The educational sites of the media and popular culture have used visual methods to merge seamlessly into schools. They have shown us the world, and acted as agents in defining children, promoted corporate interest, and delineated 'good' and 'bad'. Perhaps you do not agree with my interpretation of images; perhaps you see other images and assign them different meanings. But whatever you may see in your school space, the fact remains that pictures are telling powerful stories about childhood and *about* childhood *in* educational spaces. I have argued here that there is a dangerous mismatch between the school and the child, and some of this may be due to different systems of representation, as well as due to systems of visual misrepresentation; that we as educators need to increase our skills and fluency with visual culture; and that we need to encourage students to increase theirs. As schools are ever more infused with images and as the hue and cry of the visual world knocks on the doors of our classrooms, it becomes increasingly important that we as educators harness the vibrant power of visual communication, and that we try to find ways to engage our students in working together with us in decoding images and in producing them.

Notes
1. By 'school' here, I refer to high school. Some schools for young children are admittedly much more ocular-centric.
2. Figures are deliberately untitled.
3. *Life is Elsewhere* was the title of his popular 1976 book.
4. As I present my readings of images in schools, I do not suppose my answers or my questions to be definitive; my hope is to broadly problematize the issue. The way that images are read by different populations can, of course, vary widely. However, I believe that it is important to examine the possible readings and the intent of images circulating in schools.
5. That number (234) is dated, to the 1990s. It is reasonable to assume that currently it is higher.
6. Ironically and not surprisingly, I am unable to reproduce the images from these web pages because of copyright restrictions.
7. It is worth noting that some classes and school curriculum (in particular English Literature classes) make attempts to incorporate visual knowledge into curriculum and instruction; however, most high school instruction dismisses images.
8. I acknowledge that it is far beyond the scope of this paper to engage in a comprehensive overview of all images in classroom materials, and such an undertaking would hardly be possible.

References

Admongo.gov. 2010. http://www.admongo.gov/admongo.html.
Adweek. 2010. What kids want: A special issue. April 27. http://www.adweek.com/aw/content_display/special-reports/kids-upfront/e3ieae2fa145a05b6f7978478c58b2d84f5.
Ali-Khan, C. 2010. Common sense, uncommon knowledge and fighting words. In *Teaching against Islamaphobia*, ed. C.D. Stonebanks, J.L. Kincheloe, and S.R. Steinberg, 239–68. New York: Peter Lang.
Appadurai, A. 2008. Here and now. In *The visual culture reader*, ed. N. Mirzoeff, 2nd ed., 173–80. London/New York: Routledge.
Apple, M.W. 2001. Series editor's introduction. In *Act your age! A cultural construction of adolescence*, ed. N. Lesko, xi–xii. New York: Routledge.
Berger, J. 1972. *Ways of seeing*. London: Penguin.
Bourdieu, P. 2009. (i) Introduction. In *Media and cultural studies: Keyworks*, ed. M.G. Durham and D. Kellner, 322–8. Malden, MA: Blackwell.
Campaign for a Commercial Free Childhood. n.d. Marketing to children overview. http://www.commercialfreechildhood.org/ (accessed April 1, 2010).
Carter, R.A. 2004. Visual literacy: Critical thinking with the visual image. In *Critical thinking and learning: An encyclopedia for parents and teachers*, ed. J.L. Kincheloe and D. Weil, 291–6. Westport, CT: Greenwood Press.
Casper, M.J., and J.M. Moore. 2009. *Missing bodies: The politics of visibility*. New York: New York University Press.
Channel One Help. n.d. http://help.channelone.com/ (accessed April 3, 2010).
Chaplin, E. 2006. The convention of captioning: W.G. Sebald and the release of the captive image. *Visual Studies* 21, no. 1: 42–53.
Classmatesmarketing. n.d. http://www.classmatesmarketing.com/ (accessed April 3, 2010).
Cloud, D.L. 2008. 'To veil the threat of terror': Afghan women and the <clash of civilizations> in the imagery of the U.S. war on terrorism. In *Visual rhetoric: A reader in communication and American culture*, ed. L.C. Olson, C.A. Finnegan, and D.S. Hope, 393–412. Thousand Oaks, CA: Sage.
Consumer Union. n.d. Selling America's kids: Commercial pressures on kids of the 90's. http://www.consumersunion.org/other/sellingkids/inschoolpromo.htm (accessed April 1, 2010).
Coontz, S. 2000. *The way we never were: American families and the nostalgia trap*. New York: Persesus.
DeGennaro, D., and T. Brown. 2009. Youth voices: Connections between history, enacted culture and identity in a digital divide initiative. *Cultural Studies of Science Education* 4, no. 1: 13–39.
Flynt, E., and W. Brozo. 2010. Visual literacy and the content classroom: A question of now, not when. *Reading Teacher* 63, no. 6: 526–8.
Freire, P. 2005. *Pedagogy of the oppressed*. 30th anniversary ed. New York: Continuum International.
Freireproject.org. n.d. Joe Kincheloe interviewed. http://www.freireproject.org/content/joe-kincheloe-interviewed (accessed April 1, 2010).
Giroux, H. 2003. *The abandoned generation: Democracy beyond the culture of fear*. New York: Palgrave Macmillan.
Grosvenor, I. 2007. From the 'eye of history' to 'a second gaze': The visual archive and the marginalized in the history of education. *History of Education* 36, nos. 4–5: 607–22.
Higonnet, A. 1998. *Picture of innocence: The history and crisis of ideal childhood*. New York: Thames & Hudson.

hooks, b. 1994. *Teaching to transgress: Education as the practice of freedom.* Boston, MA: South End Press.

Kealy, W.A. 2004. Media literacy. In *Critical thinking and learning: An encyclopedia for parents and teachers*, ed. J.L. Kincheloe and D. Weil, 287–90. Westport, CT: Greenwood Press.

Kellner, D., and M.G. Durham. 2009a. Introduction to part II. In *Media and cultural studies: Keyworks*, ed. M.G. Durham and D. Kellner, 91–8. Malden, MA: Blackwell.

Kellner, D., and M.G. Durham. 2009b. Adventures in media and cultural studies: Introducing the keyworks. In *Media and cultural studies: Keyworks*, ed. M.G. Durham and D. Kellner, ix–xxxviii. Malden, MA: Blackwell.

Kenny, K. 2009. *Visual communication research designs.* New York: Routledge.

Kilbourne, J. 1999. *Can't buy my love.* New York: Touchstone.

Kincheloe, J.L. 1999. Trouble ahead, trouble behind: Grounding the post-formal critique of educational psychology. In *The post-formal reader: Cognition and education*, ed. J.L. Kincheloe, S.R. Steinberg, and P.H. Hinchey, 4–54. New York: Falmer Press.

Kincheloe, J.L. 2001. *Getting beyond the facts: Teaching social studies/social sciences in the twenty-first century.* 2nd ed. New York: Peter Lang.

Kincheloe, J.L. 2004. Home alone and bad to the bone: The advent of a postmodern childhood. In *Kinderculture: The corporate construction of childhood*, ed. S.R. Steinberg and J.L. Kincheloe, 2nd ed., 228–53. Boulder, CO: Westview.

Kincheloe, J.L. 2007. Critical pedagogy in the 21st century: Evolution for survival. In *Critical pedagogy: Where are we now?* ed. P. McLaren and J.L. Kincheloe, 9–42. New York: Peter Lang.

Kincheloe, J.L. 2009. Capital, Ray Kroc and McDonald's: The world's lovin it. In *Media/cultural studies: Critical approaches*, ed. R. Hammer and D. Kenner, 251–69. New York: Peter Lang.

Kress, T. n.d. Tilting the machine: A critique of one teacher's attempts at using art forms to create postformal, democratic learning environments. *Journal of Educational Controversy.* http://www.wce.wwu.edu/Resources/CEP/eJournal/v005n001/a008.shtml (accessed April 2, 2010).

Kress, T. 2009. In the shadow of whiteness: (Re)exploring connections between history, enacted culture, and identity in a digital divide initiative. *Cultural Studies of Science Education* 4, no. 1: 41–9.

Kundera, M. 1976. *Life is elsewhere.* New York: Knopf.

Lesko, N. 2001. *Act your age! A cultural construction of adolescence.* New York: Routledge.

Linn, S. 2005. *Consuming kids: Protecting our children from the onslaught of marketing and advertising.* New York: Anchor Books.

Margolis, E., and S. Fram. 2007. Caught napping: Images of surveillance, discipline and punishment on the body of the schoolchild. *History of Education* 36, no. 2: 191–211.

Miller, T. 2009. Children and the media: Alternative histories. In *Media/cultural studies: Critical approaches*, ed. R. Hammer and D. Kenner, 238–50. New York: Peter Lang.

Mirzoeff, N. 2008. The subject of visual culture. In *The visual culture reader*, ed. N. Mirzoeff, 2nd ed., 3–23. London/New York: Routledge.

Olson, L.C., C.A. Finnegan, and D.S. Hope. 2008. Visual rhetoric in communication: Continuing questions and contemporary issues. In *Visual rhetoric: A reader in communication and American culture*, ed. L.C. Olson, C.A. Finnegan, and D.S. Hope, 1–14. Thousand Oaks, CA: Sage.

Pedersen, C.H. 2008. Anchors of meaning – helpers of dialogue: The use of images in production of relations and meaning. *International Journal of Qualitative Studies in Education* 21, no. 1: 35–47.

P.T. Quigley.com. n.d. Company history. http://www.ptquigley.com/company.html (accessed March 21, 2010).

Rose, G. 2007. *Visual methodologies: An introduction to the interpretation of visual materials.* 2nd ed. Thousand Oaks, CA: Sage.

Sensoy, Ö. 2009. Where the heck is the 'Muslim World' anyways? In *Muslim voices in schools: Narratives of identity and pluralism*, ed. Ö. Sensoy and C.D. Stonebanks, 71–85. Rotterdam: Sense Publishers.

Sensoy, Ö. 2010. Ickity-ackity open sesame. In *Critical global perspectives: Rethinking knowledge about global societies*, ed. S. Binaya, 39–56. Charlotte, NC: Information Age.

Shaheen, J.G. 2001. *Reel bad Arabs: How Hollywood vilifies a people.* New York: Olive Branch Press.

Shor, J.B. 2004. *Born to buy.* New York: Scribner.

Steinberg, S.R. 2004. Desert minstrels: Hollywood's curriculum of Arabs and Muslims. In *The miseducation of the west: How schools and the media distort our understanding of the Islamic world*, ed. J.L. Kincheloe and S.R. Steinberg, 1–24. Westport, CT: Praeger.

Steinberg, S.R., and J.L. Kincheloe. 2004. Introduction. In *Kinderculture: The corporate construction of childhood*, ed. S.R. Steinberg and J.L. Kincheloe, 2nd ed., 1–48. Boulder, CO: Westview.

Sturken, M., and L. Cartwright. 2001. *Practices of looking: An introduction to visual culture.* New York: Oxford University Press.

Tavin, K.M. 2003. Wrestling with angels, searching for ghosts: Toward a critical pedagogy of visual culture. *Studies in Art Education* 44, no. 3: 197–213.

Time. 2003. Magazine cover. November 3. http://www.time.com/time/covers/0,16641,20031103,00.html (accessed March 23, 2010).

Time. 2007a. Magazine cover. August 27. http://www.time.com/time/covers/0,16641,20070827,00.html (accessed March 23, 2010).

Time. 2007b. Magazine cover. March 27. http://www.time.com/time/covers/0,16641,20060327,00.html (accessed March 23, 2010).

Walraven. n.d. About us. http://www.walravenco.com/bookcovers/aboutus.asp (accessed March 23, 2010).

Zoominfo. n.d. P.T. Quigley Co. http://www.zoominfo.com/Search/CompanyDetail.aspx?CompanyID=86885910&cs=QGFLcYWuU&pc=indeed (accessed April 3, 2010).

Picturing oppression: seventh graders' photo essays on racism, classism, and sexism

Özlem Sensoy

Faculty of Education, Simon Fraser University, 8888 University Drive, Burnaby, BC V5A1S6, Canada

This study, situated in an inner-city school in Western Canada, involved 20 seventh graders producing photo essays about living with racism, classism, or sexism. Two questions guided the study: (1) How do students working with a critical pedagogue conceptualize their own experiences with race, class, and gender in ways that either interrupt or reinscribe dominant mainstream curricular narratives?; and (2) To what extent can visual methods serve to open up and expand researchers' understanding of students' conceptions of their lived experiences in the context of a critical pedagogy classroom? This study drew upon critical pedagogy, critical multicultural education, and visual methodology. Issues of societal curriculum and identity were central to this work. Students' photo essays not only revealed some patterns of mainstream discourses related to race, class, and gender, but also revealed some very sophisticated understandings of how social issues play out in institutional systems.

[E]ducation should help one make sense of the world. At the same time it should help students make sense of themselves as 'players' in the world. (Kincheloe and Steinberg 1998, 2)

Introduction

Twenty seventh-graders working with a critical pedagogue participated in a month-long project in which they created photo essays that would communicate to 'the world' what it means to live with race, class, or gender oppression. This paper tells the story of this project and shares the counterstories (Delgado 1989; Nelson 2001; Sensoy and Stonebanks 2009; Solórzano and Yosso 2002a, 2002b) about race, class, and gender that the students produced.

As a population, these youth represent a diverse community. Most students speak a language other than English at home, and many are of immigrant families. They work with a teacher who is a woman of color and a graduate student completing a Masters degree, and who teaches from a critical pedagogy framework. Classroom observations and her own reporting confirm that she regularly subverts the standardized curriculum by asking students to think about the textbook as a *constructed* narrative and by bringing students' own lived experiences and concerns into the classroom.

This positioning is a central project to critical approaches to education, such as critical pedagogy and critical race theory. A 'counterstory' is defined as a narrative in which members of marginalized groups – those that have experienced oppression along a primary identity – empower and repair group and individual identities by responding to those stories generated about them in mainstream accounts (Delgado 1989; Nelson 2001; Solórzano and Yosso 2002a, 2002b). Solórzano and Yosso (2002b, 32) describe the counterstory as 'telling the stories of those people whose experiences are not often told (i.e., those on the margins of society)'. Drawing from the storytelling traditions in racialized communities, critical race scholars use counterstories or counterstorytelling (Delgado 1989) to examine how race and racism in particular have shaped the lives and experiences of students of color (Solórzano and Yosso 2002a). The value of such storytelling is the challenge such narratives can offer to mainstream accounts which often result in the muting and silencing of the stories and experiences of marginalized communities (Solórzano and Yosso 2002a, 2002b, 2002c).

Confronting mainstream narratives, such as those presented in the formal school curriculum, can itself be an act of subversion and resistance. In this context, one might expect that the 'picture' of oppression the students on the margins have would be more complex and nuanced. The students in this study were therefore uniquely situated to offer insights about how counterstories of resistance can surface, and the limits of that surfacing in a critical classroom. The research reported here is informed by the counterstory tradition and builds upon the scholarship in critical pedagogy that seeks to situate students' experiences in their *lived* worlds in ways that allow them to make sense of their world, as well as to enact their agency in that world (Freire [1970] 1993; Kincheloe and Steinberg 1998). I wanted to understand the relationship between students' lived experiences and their experiences in the classroom working with a critical pedagogue, and whether the critical work in the classroom coupled with their own experiences allowed them to go beyond mainstream discourses of multiculturalism (such as the utopia of diversity) that shape the broader school curriculum around them. Can one critical teacher 'make a difference', or are the discourses of the textbook and broader school and societal culture so powerful that they override pedagogies of transgression and reinscribe elements of neoliberal multiculturalism?

Background of the participants: the neighborhood

The students at Poppy Elementary[1] live in an economically depressed area of the Metro Vancouver region. Nearly half of the residents in this part of the city speak a language other than English or French at home, and are visible minorities (a much higher proportion than the average for the province, which is approximately one-third visible minorities). The wider neighborhood in which the school is situated is also associated with gang activity.

Low-rise, low-income housing characterizes many of the streets around the school (Figure 1). Buildings, garbage bins, playground equipment, and any other fixed surfaces are often tagged. It is not uncommon for students to walk upon sidewalks littered with garbage, including used condoms, on their way to school each morning. While a majority of the ethno-racial population of this neighborhood is White, there are large Asian heritage populations (primarily from India, Pakistan, China, Korea, and the Philippines) as well as large immigrant populations from Eastern European and former Soviet states.

Figure 1. Sidewalk adjacent to school. Photo by Reina, age 12, participant.

Poppy Elementary (Figure 2) is a K-7 public school in a school district with a total of 99 elementary schools and 19 secondary schools. As of September 2007 (the last year for which statistics are available) there were 37,892 elementary school students in the district. The school participates in various district-wide programs, including an

Figure 2. Back of school. Photo by Jie, age 12, participant.

inner-city school early literacy project, a school meal program, social development classes, and an all day ESL Kindergarten, and has an aboriginal support worker. There is a school-wide social responsibility program and performance standards, and an intervention program to help struggling readers.

From this context, the students enter Ms Chandra's classroom (Figure 3). Ms Chandra is an experienced teacher in her 30s who has been teaching for seven years. She is the child of an immigrant family to Canada, a South Asian woman, and a graduate student working on a Masters degree in equity issues in education. Her own history and social location allow her to relate to and understand many of her students' experiences in first-hand ways. She believes in integrating these experiences into the class curriculum, and often models for her students how her own life experiences (with racism, for example) are connected to bigger lessons that often lie in (or sometimes just beyond) the pages of the school curriculum or school structures. Her stories, and more often the stories that her students bring to class, routinely anchor the events of the day. For example, one day when I stopped by for an after-lunchtime visit, I walked into a class buzzing with activity. Students were huddled over classroom laptops, clicking away at the keyboards writing personal essays in response to a social controversy introduced in the class that day. I was delighted as students called me over to their monitors to read their narratives and offer support, suggestions, and praise.

Ms Chandra later told me that the class had been shocked by the percolating controversy between famous film directors Spike Lee and Clint Eastwood, about Eastwood's World War II films (*Flags of our Fathers* and *Letters from Iwo Jima*), which featured no Black characters. Students had heard that Lee had accused Eastwood of ignoring the contributions of Black soldiers to the battle at Iwo Jima. In response, Eastwood had prodded whether Lee had actually studied the history of the battle. This

Figure 3. Ms Chandra's classroom. Photo by Daniel, age 12, participant.

event had the students in Ms Chandra's class fascinated with this problem: did Hollywood film directors have a moral obligation to tell the truth when making movies about real events such as wars?

This example is illustrative of how Ms Chandra runs her class. She takes up whatever is the 'hot topic' of the day and connects it to her curriculum goals. In this case, it was an opportunity to practice the genre of persuasive essay writing. And here was a topic that the students were eager to write about.

It is in this context that I identify Ms Chandra as a critical pedagogue and her classroom as a critical classroom engaged in the issues of citizenship and social justice, as they specifically play out in the school/society relationship (Kincheloe 2001; Kincheloe and Steinberg 1998). Students are regularly invited to problematize what they hear, see, and read. This approach is grounded in a pedagogy of criticality in which mainstream modes of transmitting canonized knowledge are resisted (Banks 1996; Freire [1970] 1993; Kincheloe 2008), and the dynamics of oppression (primarily racism, classism, and sexism) are challenged. One of the key ways in which this challenge occurs is through the critiquing of mainstream curricula, often by asking questions about their positionality and production. In Ms Chandra's class, students were regularly engaged in this kind of curricular study. For example, students engaged in activities such as comparing the various accounts of a historical event like first contact and colonization in various texts: such as comparing John Smith and Pocahontas as characters in the Disney story from the film *Pocahontas*, with actual historical information about John Smith and Pocahontas, as well as the various accounts of Indigenous/Colonizer contact that students have access to in their school textbook. By examining the differences between various representations, students engaged in a study of how stories about people and knowledge about historical events come to be constructed, and the manner in which some knowledge is legitimized and 'made official' while other knowledge is left in the proverbial dustbins of historical archives.

Method and procedures

Ms Chandra's grade seven class is demographically representative of the school at large (see Table 1). There were 24 students in the class. Fifteen of these students were on IEPs (individual education plans that are modified to support students with special needs or modified expectations for performance).

This study was approved by the researcher's university ethics review board, as well as the school district and school in which the work was carried out. Parents and families were informed in writing and via conversations with the classroom teacher about the project. All 24 students were given cameras and participated in the project; 20 returned the requisite permissions forms and gave consent to have their work be part of the research. Of the 20 students, 15 completed a photo essay. The demographics of the students in the classroom are in Table 1 (these demographics are based on a combination of students' self-identification and details that Ms Chandra thought relevant to the students' identities).

Of the 20 participating students, 11 males and 9 females, 13 were born in a country other than Canada and an additional two who were born in Canada are of Aboriginal ancestry. Twelve speak a language other than English.

I began my work with Ms Chandra's students by informally visiting the class. I was introduced as one of Ms Chandra's teachers from the university. I spent a few weeks stopping by for short visits – usually on Thursdays after lunch. I would sit in

Table 1. Demographics of the students who gave consent.

1. Daniel (M) age 12	Born in Canada, White, Western European heritage	Speaks English
2. Xue (M) age 13	Born in China, Asian heritage	Speaks Chinese and English
3. Cora (F) age 13	Born in Canada, White heritage	Speaks English
4. Amir (M) age 14	Born in Iraq, Arab Christian heritage	ESL student, speaks Arabic
5. Kofi (M) age 12	Born in Zimbabwe, Black heritage	Speaks English, Shona, and Ndebele
6. Bronte (F) age 12	Born in Canada, White, Western European heritage	Speaks English
7. Allison (F) age 13	Born in Canada, White, Western European heritage	Speaks English
8. Cruz (M) age 12	Born in Philippines, Filipino heritage	Speaks English and Tagalog
9. Latif (M) age 12	Born in Germany, Albanian Muslim heritage	Speaks English and Albanian
10. Amaro (M) age 12	Born in Canada, Aboriginal heritage	Speaks English
11. Ahn (M) age 12	Born in Myanmar, fled to Thailand and raised in refugee camp	ESL student, speaks Burmese
12. Na'ila (F) age 13	Born in Japan, Japanese and Arab heritage	Speaks English
13. Macawi (F) age 12	Born in Canada, Aboriginal heritage	Speaks English
14. WenYan (M) age 13	Born in South Korea, South Korean heritage	Speaks English and Korean
15. Jie (M) age 12	Born in China, Chinese heritage	Speaks English and Chinese
16. Reina (F) age 13	Born in Philippines, Filipina heritage	Speaks English and Tagalog
17. Kiyet (M) age 12	Born in Thailand, Burmese heritage	Speaks English and Burmese
18. Wera (F) age 13	Born in Poland, Polish heritage	Speaks English and Polish
19. Ajaya (F) age 13	Born in Canada, Black Caribbean heritage	Speaks English
20. Adrina (F) age 12	Born in Indonesia, Indonesian heritage	Speaks English and Malay

and engage as work was being done – everything from essay writing to after-school practice of the cheers students were writing for the track meet. After several weeks of informal visits, allowing students to become familiar with my presence, Ms Chandra and I shared with them a visual puzzle to get us started on examining the power of images. I created a color photocopy of the famous photograph of the 'unknown rebel' at Tiananmen Square in 1989, by photographer Jeff Widener.[2]

Each student was given a color photocopy of Widener's photograph to take home (without identifiers as to the event, location, or who took the photograph). Over the weekend, their job was to examine the photograph and think about two questions: What is this photograph about? What do pictures mean? The goal of these questions was for students to think about the metaphorical (as compared to simply the literal) aspects of representations and also to have a concrete (and famous) example of what is widely acknowledged as a powerful photograph in order to practice thinking about the role of visual discourse.

While a less often used method in education (Clark-Ibáñez 2004; Vinson and Ross 2003), image-based methods have had a longer history in sociological and anthropological research (c.f. Collier and Collier 1986; Harper 1993; Prosser 1998; Pink 2006; Rose 2001; Thomson 2008). Image-based research in education most often takes the form of content and discourse analysis of images (e.g., Magno and Kirk 2008; Sensoy 2010; Sensoy and DiAngelo 2006); or strategies for enhancing qualitative approaches such as interviews via photo-elicitation (e.g., Clark-Ibáñez 2004; Sensoy and DiAngelo 2006). This image-based research also includes visual documentation of ethnographic sites or methods described as photo-voice or auto-photography, in which subjects are given cameras with which to document their environment and experiences (e.g., Brown 2005; Noland 2006).

A visual methods approach was appealing for at least two reasons: first, photography and visual content made this project more accessible to this high ESL and high IEP population of students and allowed for a new forum within the formal school structure that complemented the traditional classroom work occurring in the school. Second, critical methodologists have argued that to explain the social world is fundamentally a 'messy' business (Denzin and Lincoln 2000; Kincheloe and Berry 2004; Law 2004). Therefore, the use of visual methods (such as photo essays) may offer new ways of capturing this messy business and the complexity of social realities as they relate to race, class, and gender. Doing so, without falling victim to what Law (2004) describes as distorting the messy social world into clarity, is not simply a goal for researchers, but a way of thinking complexly about the world that we want young people to practice and understand. Grounded in these commitments and prepared to take on the 'mess' of kids' ideas about race, class, and gender in their lives, the photo projects began. The goals were two-fold: to allow students a creative venue by which to produce their own counterstories and to explore if and how students bridged their knowledge derived from critical classroom work about race, class, and gender with their own lived experiences.

Back to the classroom

In the case of our photo challenge, the results were profoundly effective. One student (Jie) returned to school after the weekend to report that he had a personal connection to the picture. His father had been at Tiananmen Square on the day the photo was taken, and was able to identify 'the June 4th Incident'. The students in the class were both surprised and in awe. The photograph had given Jie and his dad an opportunity to talk about a historical moment and connect their family's lived experience to school in a powerful way. Jie and his dad became the equivalent of rock stars, and the students became excited by Jie's discovery and eager to learn more about photographs.

Harnessing this excitement, Ms Chandra and I shared the project's goal with the students: that we wanted to see how they combined their school-based work with their own real-life experiences and knowledge. The students were invited to participate in a photo essay project in which they took photographs and then produced a photo essay telling the story of 'living with' race, class, or gender. Here, briefly, are the instructions students were given.

> Before you begin, think about:
>
> What messages do I see around me about race (such as home language or religion or ethnicity) … or messages about class (including topics such as poverty or wealth or success) … or messages about gender (such as what it means to act like a boy or act like a girl)?
>
> What will your photo essay be about? What would you like others to know about living with classism, or living with racism, or living with sexism. What images come to your mind when you think about race, class, and gender?
>
> You have spent many months now studying social issues, such as racism, classism, and sexism. You will now produce a photo essay to show how these issues relate to your own life.
>
> Photographs and photo essays are frequently used in research in which people want to tell a story with pictures. It is a way to express real-life experiences.
>
> You must:
>
> (1) take up to 27 photos of objects, places, settings, and groups of people;
> (2) only use the disposable digital camera you are given;
> (3) complete the assignment by yourself to the best of your abilities. Do not ask others to take photographs for you; and
> (4) complete the assignment by Monday, you only have the current weekend
>
> As photographers we must always be respectful with our subjects – whether they are people, places, or things. Do not alter or disturb anything you take a photograph of. Please always remain respectful.
>
> You CAN take photographs of people who are outdoors and in public places without their permission;
>
> You CANNOT take photographs of people who are in private places (such as malls) because we would have to obtain their permission;
>
> DO NOT take close-up photographs of individuals;
>
> DO NOT take photographs of situations or circumstances that would be intrusive, embarrassing to anyone, or create false impressions.
>
> Dr Sensoy will review all your photographs. Any pictures you take that seem to be intrusive or not-respectful (either intentionally or by mistake) will be destroyed, and you will not be allowed to use it in your photo essay.
>
> Any pictures you take with people in them will be examined to ensure the people's faces are not identifiable. Any image in which the people are potentially identifiable will be altered digitally before you can use it in your photo essay.
>
> Have fun!

It is important to clarify that all the students were familiar with the language of 'racism', 'sexism', and 'classism', since Ms Chandra had been utilizing this language in the classroom all year. Thus, by the end of the school year, which is when the project took place (in May), the students were not new to the discourse of racism, classism, and sexism.

After instructions, students were each given a disposable camera and a period of three days (from Friday to Monday) to take their pictures. I picked up the cameras mid-week and returned the following week with two sets of printouts and a CD for each student containing digital versions of her/his photographs. The students got to keep one print set of the photographs they took. Even if students did not want their work to be part of the research project, all the students in class were given disposable cameras to take pictures with and had their photographs developed.

The next step in the project was for students to decide on 'the story' they wanted to tell about living with racism, living with classism, or living with sexism. They spent an afternoon sprawled out on the floor and table-tops of the classroom laying out their photographs and deciding which ones to use (Figure 4). Then, students wrote text to go along with the images and selected music from a free online music database.

The students spent only two formal class sessions loading their digital photographs, music, and narrative texts into Apple's iMovie program (which was the program loaded on the school's laptops in the laptop cart used for classroom work). Luckily, the Vice Principal at the school, Mr Wilson, had a graduate degree in educational technology and loved the idea of the technology component. He came by to give the students a tutorial and help troubleshoot technical problems students might be having. Many of the students spent additional time working on their photo essays either in the computer lab, or during free time in the classroom.

Figure 4. Students working on photo selection. Photo by Özlem.

Findings

Students were asked to focus their photo essays on one of the three themes: race, class, or gender. Five students (one female and four males) picked the theme of race, eight students (3F and 5M) picked class, and six (4F and 2M) picked gender. In what follows, I share the most striking features of their work.

Theme 1: Thinking literally, thinking metaphorically

Many of the photographs students took were not specific to any theme, were too unfocused to use, or were 'double tries' at capturing an image. Students had varying degrees of comfort working with cameras, and students worked together at times taking photographs of the same objects. Despite this, an observable pattern that was not surprising was the *literal* interpretation of the themes. For instance, if their theme was race, students took photographs of skin and hair, such as shown in Figure 5.

If the theme was gender, students took photographs of objects that marked gender, such as sports caps and make-up (Figure 6).

And if the theme was class, there were photos of 'stuff', such as money, brand name designer labels, and 'high-class' markers such as wine glasses (Figure 7).

Ahn's full photo essay is a good illustration of how a literal interpretation about race was taken up by students. This is the URL for Ahn's photo essay, 'Different Colors': http://www.youtube.com/watch?v=KWWCirw1OYU. The text of Ahn's photo essay reads:

Different Colours
Different Skin Colours
Different Hair Colours

Figure 5. Ahn (theme: race).

Figure 6. Cora (theme: gender).

Figure 7. Na'ila (theme: class).

Different Shades of Colour
Different Hair Textures: Curly and Blond, Black and Straight
Different Hair Colours: Brown, Auburn, and Black

This type of interpretation is important because it gives educators insights into the discourses students are most fluent in. When asked to 'picture' what race is, or the story of race, Ahn (and many other students) produced a literal image. Perhaps, this presentation is also related to students' knowledge about what it is socially desirable to produce in school work. That is, being familiar with the normative codes of school, students such as Ahn produced work that they deemed would be 'right'.

However, noteworthy were several photographs and photo essays that bridged into a metaphorical representational discourse around race, class, and gender. Latif, a student of Albanian Muslim heritage, took this photograph (Figure 8) and developed his idea about race based on what this meant to him.

A new Canadian of Albanian heritage, Latif is both Muslim and White. This dual identity (or 'disguise' as he called it) gave him a complex social location. Latif's full photo essay, 'Take a Walk in my Shoes', is available at this URL: http://www.youtube.com/watch?v=gwTPgtb2xGI. The text of Latif's photo essay, which accompanies the images, reads:

Take a walk in my shoes they are two sizes too small.
Two of the same bears but going through two different struggles.
You see how I walk that thin line? It's very difficult.
The world doesn't understand what they made people go through.
Being treated poorly is something I have come to accept.
But my disguise makes me more fortunate than others.
Think harder before you judge.

Figure 8. Latif (theme: race).

Metaphorical storytelling (referring to the 'thin line' walked as someone who experiences both White privilege and simultaneously Islamophobia), was presented over images of white and brown teddy bears (the 'same bears' referred to in his text), which, although side by side, go through two different struggles. When talking about his photo essay, Latif described how even though his family is perceived as White, it is more complicated than that, since his mom wears a hijab, and their family is often profiled when traveling.

Theme 2: I want them to 'feel' what it's like

Other aspects of metaphorical versus literal storytelling occurred in Kofi's photo essay. Unlike other students who chose several photographs to tell their stories, Kofi worked primarily with a single photograph (Figure 9).

In his photo essay, 'Living with Racism: Me and the World', http://www.youtube.com/watch?v=kHaZvcZafzQ, Kofi told this story:

> Do you see the light fluffy clouds?
> Do you see the bright blue sky?
> Do you see the sun's reflection?
> Do you see how the colours around the ring are just like the moon?
> Do you see how the sun reflects on to the steel?
> Or, do you just see the colour of my skin?

Kofi's essay ends powerfully, with the sound of a strong heartbeat heard while the image fades to black. When describing his essay, Kofi said that he wanted people who saw it to *experience* 'what it feels like' – his understanding that as a dark-skinned Black youth, his skin color is the first and immediate thing that people notice about him.

Figure 9. Kofi (theme: race).

Many other students who wanted the audience to *think*, *stop*, or *feel* did not want to make it easy for the audience. For example, Cruz chose a small font for his iMovie. The theme of Cruz's essay was social class. Cruz's photo essay, 'Living with Classism: Wonders of Wealth', is available here: http://www.youtube.com/watch?v=MtsgSZCbrjc. When asked by Ms Chandra about the size and whether it may be too small on a small screen, Cruz spent quite a bit of time thinking about the problem. Then he decided to keep the small font size because, in his words, he wanted the audience to 'work' to understand his essay. The goal for Cruz and other students who wanted to 'push' the audience was to make the audience more unsettled, uncomfortable, and work harder at understanding race, class, or gender.

As Latif prompts his audience, 'Think harder before you judge'. In another photo essay (focused on gender), Kiet concludes with a similar call against judgment. He writes:

> I am not a fighter, so I am called a wuss
> I am not an athlete, so I am called a newbie
> I do not feel the connection, so I am called an outsider
> I am a caretaker, but I am not a sissy
> Wuss, weakling, helpless, wimp, sissy, feminine
> This is not who I am
> Kind-hearted, compassionate, caring, helpful, friendly, emotional, funny, happy-go-lucky
> Do not judge me

Kiet's photo essay, 'Living with Gender Stereotypes: I am not who you think I am supposed to be', is available at: http://www.youtube.com/watch?v=5xY6uQ48rBc.

While the metaphorical potential of images was a theme among some essays, and the literal interpretation of race (as skin and hair), class (as poverty and littering), and gender (as make up and baseball caps) was dominant in most essays, the *emotional* aspects of the majority of the essays cannot be over-stated. Students posed extremely powerful questions in their essays, such as WenYan, who examined the cultural gap between his upper-class life in South Korea and his new life in Canada and wrote, 'Sometimes I feel like I don't belong here' (http://www.youtube.com/watch?v=Q5u3Q8xO-nE), or Wera, who in her essay on conformity to gender norms to be pretty asked, 'Do I have to be the same to fit in?' (http://www.youtube.com/watch?v=iESNWwlXYAg), or Daniel, who explored his non-athletic body not matching his love for playing basketball and asked, 'Do you think I can shoot a free throw?' (http://www.youtube.com/watch?v=2y11-wlpfKw).

Theme 3: Unsettled expertise

A final noteworthy theme to emerge from this work was the way that photographic and movie production work unsettled the identifications of who were the academic 'high' and 'low' achievers in the class. Students who could be considered high achievers via traditional measures (such as test scores) tended to struggle with this assignment, while those who would be considered low achievers via traditional measures seemed to do well, and in some cases even flourished with the task.

Three students in particular illustrated this unsettling of traditional notions of intelligence and achievement. By many accounts, Na'ila is the smartest kid in class, a super achiever who is on the university track. Na'ila struggled with virtually every aspect of this project, asking at every element, 'Am I doing it right?' Na'ila took the required number of photographs, most of which fell into the 'literal' interpretation of her chosen theme of class, such as photographs of money (Figure 7 above), garbage (Figure 10), and jewelry (Figure 11).

Figure 10. Na'ila (theme: class).

Figure 11. Na'ila (theme: class).

Na'ila did not complete a photo essay that she was happy with. Throughout the project, she was visibly frustrated.

On the other hand, Amaro was one of the students in the class who was often absent and considered to be a low achiever. While he did not have time to complete his photo essay, Amaro's photographs were among the most visually compelling. The theme he chose was class. He was the only student who did not take photographs of people but rather objects and the landscape. Figures 12 and 13 are examples of Amaro's photographs.

Similarly, Wera illustrated another challenge to traditional notions of achievement and expertise. She was an unpopular student, not particularly 'girly' by her own photo essay exploration, and a social outsider. She only took 15 photographs, many of which were unusable because they were too blurry. However, Wera became an 'expert' in using iMovie, often assisting us (Özlem, Ms Chandra, and the Vice Principal Mr Wilson) in troubleshooting the technical problems other students were having.

There was not time in the project to follow up with Na'ila about her frustrations, or Amaro about his photographic decision-making, or Wera about her tech know-how. The work in the classroom occurred at the end of the school year when daily

Figure 12.   Amaro (theme: class).

Figure 13. Amaro (theme: class).

interruptions for assemblies, special field trips, and track meets were the norm. But what these observations reveal are some important next steps in what and how we teach about issues related to race, class, and gender, and how we recognize the development of thinking related to race, class, and gender.

Conclusion
Beginning this project, I wanted to understand the relationship between students' lived experiences and their experiences in the classroom working with a critical pedagogue, and whether the critical work in the classroom coupled with their own experiences allowed them to go beyond mainstream discourses of diversity around them. Specifically, I wanted to understand the ways in which one critical pedagogue could 'make a difference' in the types of narratives about race, class, and gender that students produced, especially given the profound personal experience many of them have 'on the margins'. Perhaps not surprisingly, the discourses of the broader school and societal culture of neoliberal multiculturalism were strong. They were evidenced by the superficial characteristics of race, class, and gender that many of the students anchored their projects in, and the messages of unity and oneness that characterized many of the essays. Further, students' own racial, class, or gender positionings were not reliable indicators of more complex storytelling about race, class, or gender issues.

There were also methodological limitations. We were up against the school calendar at the end of the year when 'regular' classroom activities are often interrupted for special assemblies, early summer trips to the amusement park, and sports festivities. Because of this, there was no time to do any formal interviews with any of the students. Most of the references to student ideas reported here are based on discussions had with students while they were working on their essays in class. Thus, there are some limits to what we can infer about their ideas about how they may have (or may not have) been bringing their personal experiences or complex stories to their essays.

Despite these very real limitations and challenges, the counterstories produced by these students have revealed some important avenues for deeper examination. First, students' experiences in the classroom working on issues of race, class, and gender with a critical pedagogue were not reliable indicators for a more complex presentation of race, class, and gender. The students were asked to focus their essays on one of these three social locations because of their familiarity with the language of 'race, class, and gender', as they had spent the year using this language with their teacher. What is compelling about the counterstories they produced is not so much the insights they offer about students' ideas on race, class, or gender, but the capacity (or limitations) of students to integrate their lived experience and knowledge with school-based knowledge. Despite the opportunity for non-linear and non-literal storytelling that the medium of photography and movie-making offer, most students in the class as a whole did not engage with storytelling that extended beyond the *literal* (e.g., the literal elements of race, class, or gender identifiers that are prominent in mainstream accounts). There may be reasons for this, including students' unfamiliarity with the media, lack of time, and perhaps not enough establishment of a comfort level with the investigator to allow for more 'creative' and non-mainstream expressions to emerge. Also, it is possible that despite the teacher's regular classroom norms, this was seen as a 'school' project, and so the discourses of school (the socially acceptable discourses related to diversity) were produced. Still, these explanations do not account for those students who *did* produce more transgressive essays. For example, those students who made deliberate choices about making audiences 'work hard' to understand an experience of racism, or those students who worked at communicating a 'feeling' associated with race, class, or gender experiences. Or those students who took photographs that were far outside the norms of the photographs taken by other students.

What these observations reveal is at least two things: first, that the mainstream curriculum (in school and beyond) is a pervasive and powerful force even when students are invited to 'free think' and develop their own stories about their own experiences. This pervasiveness in some cases cannot override the work of a critical teacher who has spent the bulk of a school year working with students to use the language of racism, sexism, and classism, to integrate their own social experiences, and to practice critical thinking and inquiry into how knowledge is constructed in school curricula. Second, students' own race, class, or gender locations – especially if they are marked as belonging to a marginalized group – were not a reliable predictor of complex storytelling. Thus a question emerges: if the readings of the essays that I have identified as transgressive can be widely concurred as such, then what common denominator do those students bring? All of the transgressive productions were produced by students who did, indeed, occupy a location on the 'margin' of mainstream social life. However, so did other students whose essays would not be characterized as transgressive.

One possibility is the metaphorical and emotional opportunities that emerge in visual storytelling. All of the student essays and photographs that could be viewed as transgressive shared an emotional call or metaphorical complexity. However with only 20 participants and 15 completed essays, there are not enough numbers in the pool of participants to speculate about a common ground. Despite this challenge of numbers, however, the potential of ongoing visual work with students to get at the emotional layers, and the metaphorical layers of race, class, and gender, cannot be ignored. What is compelling and relevant about this emotional layer in the texts is the insight they offer into the non-emotional and predominantly cerebral aspects of the traditional classroom.

Among the key goals of a critical pedagogy are to facilitate kids' examination and understanding of the world and to problematize mainstream knowledge and discourses. Ongoing questions about the potential of visual work with students may bring new insights about how this work can occur.

Notes
1. School, teacher, and student names are all pseudonyms.
2. We were unable to acquire the funds required to reproduce the image here; any Internet search engine will produce the famous Widener photo.

References

Banks, J.A., ed. 1996. *Multicultural education, transformative knowledge, and action: Historical and contemporary perspectives.* New York: Teachers College Press.

Brown, E.L. 2005. Using photography to explore hidden realities and raise cross-cultural sensitivity in future teachers. *Urban Review* 37, no. 2: 149–71.

Clark-Ibáñez, M. 2004. Framing the social world with photo-elicitation interviews. *American Behavioral Scientist* 47, no. 12: 1507–27.

Collier, J., and M. Collier. 1986. *Visual anthropology: Photography as a research method.* Albuquerque, NM: University of New Mexico Press.

Delgado, R. 1989. Storytelling for oppositionists and others: A plea for narrative. *Michigan Law Review* 87, no. 8: 2411–41.

Denzin, N.K., and Y.S. Lincoln. 2000. *Handbook of qualitative research.* 2nd ed. Thousand Oaks, CA: Sage.

Freire, P. [1970] 1993. *Pedagogy of the oppressed.* New York: Continuum.

Harper, D. 1993. On the authority of the image: Visual sociology at the crossroads. In *Handbook of qualitative sociology*, ed. N.K. Denzin and Y.S. Lincoln, 403–12. Thousand Oaks, CA: Sage.

Kincheloe, J.L. 2001. *Getting beyond the facts: Teaching social studies/social sciences in the twenty-first century.* 2nd ed. New York: Peter Lang.

Kincheloe, J.L. 2008. *Knowledge and critical pedagogy: An introduction.* Montreal: Springer Press.

Kincheloe, J.L., and K.S. Berry. 2004. *Rigour and complexity in educational research: Conceptualizing the bricolage.* Maidenhead: Open University Press.

Kincheloe, J.L., and S.R. Steinberg. 1998. *Students as researchers: Creating classrooms that matter.* Bristol, PA: Falmer Press.

Law, J. 2004. *After method: Mess in social science research.* New York: Routledge.

Magno, C., and J. Kirk. 2008. Imaging girls: Visual methodologies and messages for girls' education. *Compare* 38, no. 3: 349–62.

Nelson, H.L. 2001. *Damaged identities, narrative repair.* Ithaca, NY: Cornell University Press.

Noland, C.M. 2006. Auto-photography as research practice: Identity and self-esteem research. *Journal of Research Practice* 2, no. 1. http://jrp.icaap.org/index.php/jrp/article/view/19/65.

Pink, S. 2006. *The future of visual anthropology: Engaging the senses.* New York: Routledge.
Prosser, J., ed. 1998. *Image-based research: A sourcebook for qualitative researchers.* New York: Routledge.
Rose, G. 2001. *Visual methodologies.* Thousand Oaks, CA: Sage.
Sensoy, Ö. 2010. Ickity ackity open sesame: Learning about the Middle East in images. In *Rethinking curricular knowledge on global societies,* ed. B. Subedi, 39–55. Charlotte, NC: Information Age Publishing.
Sensoy, Ö., and R. DiAngelo. 2006. 'I wouldn't want to be a woman in the Middle East': White female narratives of Muslim oppression. *Radical Pedagogy* 8, no. 1. http://radicalpedagogy.icaap.org/content/issue8_1/sensoy.html.
Sensoy, Ö., and C.D. Stonebanks. 2009. Introduction: Voice and other acts of insubordination. In *Muslim voices in school: Narratives of identity and pluralism*, ed. Ö. Sensoy and C.D. Stonebanks, ix–xx. Boston, MA: Sense Publishers.
Solórzano, D.G., and T.J. Yosso. 2002a. A critical race counterstory of race, racism, and affirmative action. *Equity & Excellence in Education* 35, no. 2: 155–68.
Solórzano, D.G., and T.J. Yosso. 2002b. Critical race methodology: Counter-storytelling as an analytical framework for education research. *Qualitative Inquiry* 8, no. 1: 23–44.
Solórzano, D.G., and T.J. Yosso. 2002c. Maintaining social justice hopes within academic realities: A Freirean approach to critical race/LatCrit pedagogy. *Denver Law Review* 78, no. 4: 595–621.
Thomson, P., ed. 2008. *Doing visual research with children and young people.* New York: Routledge.
Vinson, K.D., and E.W. Ross. 2003. *Image and education: Teaching in the face of the new disciplinarity.* New York: Peter Lang.

'Working with' as a methodological stance: collaborating with students in teaching, writing, and research

Christina A. Siry[a] and Elizabeth Zawatski[b]

[a]Faculty of Language and Literature, Humanities, Arts and Education, University of Luxembourg, Walferdange, Luxembourg; [b]Ox Ridge School, Darien Public Schools, Darien, CT, USA

> Using critical ethnography guided by cultural sociology, this paper examines the role of 'co' in teacher education; coresearching, coteaching, and cogenerating dialogue. The authors are a pre-service teacher and a college instructor, and through our multiple perspectives and positionings, we explore how collaboration served to dismantle teacher–student hierarchies and replaced them with complex relationships mediated by polysemic approaches to research. Pushing against traditional ideologies, we utilize a multi-voiced approach to writing as we present our experiences and interpretations of data relative to the possibilities of collaboration in education and research. As we analyze our role in collaborative endeavors, we ask: How can we find ways to work *across* and *around* hierarchical institutional structures when working with our students? What are ways that we can examine our individual lived experiences together, and is it possible to work with each other to develop identities as teachers that are not predicated on power differentials?

Introduction

> Before this course, I was one of those people who thought of taking a course (and of teaching) as an individual endeavor. I never thought of it any other way because it was how I experienced teaching in all the courses I had taken. I can remember thinking about how annoyed I was that I was going to have to work with other students in this class, especially those I didn't know. I imagined them being lazy or uncooperative. Anything that <u>could</u> go wrong with a partnership I imagined <u>would</u> happen in my experiences working with the other students. I remember thinking about the amount of time it would take to meet and discuss, even after Chris said we would do most of the planning together in class time. However, once the course began and I began to collaborate, the negatives I had imagined began to dissipate and I realized how beneficial it was to have someone to bounce ideas off of. (Beth, journal entry)

This paper is about 'working with' others in classrooms. In the above reflection, Beth (a pre-service teacher) writes about her experiences as a participant in a field-based science methods course that incorporates collaborative teaching and planning as central components of learning to teach. We, the authors of this paper, were participants in this course in the fall of 2007. Chris (the first author) was the instructor, and Beth (the second author) was a student. Within this course, participants met twice weekly; with one session devoted to coteaching science to children in an elementary school and a second session occurring on campus to engage in dialogue around our experiences in the classroom. Science teaching was a shared event, as we all worked together to develop a unit that we then taught collaboratively within the same elementary classroom on a weekly basis for one semester.

This critically oriented research, and the teaching in the course in which the research was conducted, are driven by one central question: How can we find ways in education and educational research to work *across* and *around* hierarchical institutional structures when working with our students? We have wondered, what are the ways that we can examine our individual lived experiences together, and is it possible to work with each other to develop identities as teachers that are not predicated on power differentials? Our opening vignette situates our primary focus on shared responsibility through collaborative methods. In the sections that follow, we examine specific ways we approached teaching together, researching together, and learning together, and we elaborate on collaboration as a methodological stance to push against existing hierarchical structures of teacher > student, researcher > researched, and self > other.[1] We detail how a collaborative approach served to work towards achieving polysemicity and highlighting difference, and we discuss how we learned about each other and learned about teaching. Ultimately, we draw pedagogical implications for teacher education courses as a place to deconstruct the notions of 'teacher' and 'student' and emphasize the multiplicity of perspectives in classrooms while supporting the co-construction of relationships built upon learning together.

Situating our study: a collaborative field-based framework to learning to teach

Elementary classrooms are multifaceted, unique contexts, and teaching and learning are extremely complex processes. The field of teacher education has long been trying to prepare pre-service teachers for the complexities of teaching and learning. One approach has been to situate teacher preparation 'in the field' of classrooms. Our research examines field-based experiences for pre-service teachers within a methods course designed to be partially based in an elementary classroom. Off-campus methods courses are not new, and the call for courses to emphasize interactions that approximate what might be found in real teaching situations has existed for decades (e.g. Drumheller and Paris 1966; Ashenfelter and Hanson 1971). However, despite substantial literature concerning field experiences and practica for pre-service teachers (e.g., ten Dam and Blom 2006), there is surprisingly little recent literature that concerns field-based methods courses specifically.

Many programs have clinical experience or practica, yet they rarely provide opportunities for pre-service teachers to teach *with* their colleagues in schools. Our study focuses on a methods course in particular and examines the role of cotaught lessons in which all course members participate in teaching and, thus, in learning to teach science together in classrooms. As the opening reflection alludes to, in these *collaborative field-based science methods courses* participants work together to develop lessons to teach to elementary-aged children. In the teaching of the science lessons, the course participants (including Chris, the instructor) work together in the same classroom. These shared teaching experiences then provide the basis for critical, reflexive analyses of children's learning and our teaching, as interpretations of events are discussed by members of the group in cogenerative dialogues (Tobin and Roth 2006). Cogenerative dialogues are a key structure to this course, as these conversations provide the opportunity for reflexively considering shared experiences with the explicit purpose of revealing different perspectives and considering plans of action to improve teaching and learning.

Pushing back on reductionist teacher 'training'

Current pressures in teacher education policy are creating a trend away from equity-oriented, professionalized approaches to learning how to teach and towards a renewed focus on teacher-as-technician approaches that define teaching in terms of discrete skills and testable knowledge (Sleeter 2008). Teacher education is dominated by an emphasis on measurable outcomes and skills, often with a specific focus on preparing children to be successful on standardized tests. This reliance on steps and processes frames teaching as a low-skill activity and reduces teaching to passing on a set of discrete facts and limited meanings to be reproduced (Kincheloe 2003). In these reductionistic approaches to teacher education, pre-service teachers 'are often preoccupied with learning the "how to", with "what works" or with mastering the best way to teach a given body of knowledge' (Giroux 2004, 208). Rather than attempting to reconstruct a given set of facts, the teacher education course that we write about herein is based upon the view that meanings reside within and through collective relationships and interactions. With that understanding and by collaborating to construct experiences within an education course, participants can be supported in producing knowledge about teaching and learning together. In doing so, they are positioned to critically push back against the forces that assume that standards and strict accountability equate with gaining knowledge.

The overlapping experience of co-constructing a field-based course and co-constructing research around the course is our focus in this paper, as we posit alternatives to teacher 'training' and traditional hierarchical structures. Maxine Greene (1995) emphasizes that seeking alternatives might lead to new approaches as: 'once we can see our givens as contingencies, then we may have an opportunity to posit alternative ways of living and valuing and to make choices' (23). Our collaborations occurred through a combination of the field-based course and a subsequent research group that examined what was accomplished within the course. Greene's emphasis on making choices connects with the focus of the course and our collaborative research, as it is in creating opportunities for teachers to explore and develop their own strategies to engage students in meaningful, relevant work that we seek alternatives to the status quo. In this search for alternatives, we can counter the false notion that teaching methods can be removed from the subject being taught and that this in turn can be removed from processes occurring within classrooms.

The complexities of collaboration

Key to our experiences is that they are based on collaboration. Distinct from cooperation, in which individual efforts are generally accomplished side-by-side, collaboration refers to the work of a diverse group focused on coordinating individual efforts to complete a common task and to complete it together (Ares 2008). Within educational research specifically, a focus on collaboration can bring diverse perspectives to interpretation and subvert the false notion of a single truth (Siry and Ali-Khan, forthcoming). The phrase '*working with*' in this paper's title illustrates the methodological, pedagogical foundation of collaboration emphasized through our framework to a field-based methods course. Cogenerative dialogues, coteaching, and coresearching all served as approaches for collaboration during and after the course. Cogenerative dialogues are structured discussions between participants in educational situations, generally with a focus on improving practice. Cogenerative dialogues can afford opportunities to 'identify and review what seems to work and what does not, especially practices and schema that disadvantage participants' (Tobin and Roth 2006, 81). They have been transformative in a wide variety of teaching and learning situations, including for resolving conflict in classrooms (Martin 2005), expanding roles by positioning students as researchers (Elmesky and Tobin 2005), and as professional development and evaluation of in-service teachers (Martin and Scantlebury 2009). Coteaching connects with cogenerative dialogue as together these approaches provide the opportunity for teachers to reflexively consider events they have shared with the purpose of improving teaching.[2]

Our explicit focus on working together to co-construct science teaching experiences emphasizes a two-fold perspective: first, the desire to understand the perspectives of others, and second, the focus on learning by assuming (and sharing) responsibility for teaching and learning. Dialogical encounters structured around collaboration are intended to push against the institutionally embedded notions of the role of 'teacher' and the role of 'student', as it is the students who construct the teaching and learning experiences.

Within this particular collaborative field-based framework, coteaching and cogenerative dialogue have been shown to facilitate collective responsibility for teaching science (Siry and Lowell, forthcoming) and for supporting new teachers' developing sense of themselves as professionals (Siry et al. 2010). Further, this structure mediated pre-service teachers' identities as new teachers of science and their sense of belonging and solidarity (Siry 2009). Herein, we narrow and deepen our interpretive focus to consider the specific ways this process generated and was generated by a methodological, epistemological approach to plurality grounded in the complexities of collaboration.

Producing knowledge on learning to teach together

We utilize cowriting to highlight what happened within our course from personal, individual perspectives. In working towards a polyvocality within writing and research, we often write from a voice of 'we'. However, we stress that part of our epistemology requires the seeking of a plurality of perspectives and requires recognizing individual differences. Through our polyvocality, we emphasize working towards polysemicity that acknowledges and welcomes difference. For that reason, we intentionally interrupt the textual voice of *we* with the voice of *I*, and textboxes serve to set off these perspectives as we seek to 'disrupt the narrative of "we" with the thoughts of the "I"' (Siry and Ali-Khan, forthcoming). These distinctive written voices highlight the multiple, situated, shifting positions and perspectives that we hold at any given time and come together *around* and *as* data to analyze and interpret as we draw connections. Collaborative co-writing is what Dorothy Lander and Leona English (2000) refer to as 'second-person knowing' (346) – coming to know the other so that there can be a search for understanding across difference. As we collaboratively produced knowledge on our experiences through this paper, transcript excerpts guided our writing. We present moments that have passed and layer upon these our current responses within textboxes, as we theorize together the ways this process emphasized the plurality of experiences and the value of communicating across difference. We stress that no moment can be captured and re/presented completely and in the retelling and reframing, it always becomes something new.

The research project: contextualizing 'us'

This is a study of lived experiences, and hermeneutic phenomenology shed light on the contextual aspects of individual experiences and provided a meaningful way to represent and learn about experiences. Phenomenology describes how one orients to lived experience; hermeneutics describes how one interprets the 'texts' of life. A hermeneutic approach seeks a 'fusion of horizons' (Gadamer 2004), with a horizon being all that we can 'see' from where we are as historically and culturally situated individuals. As people come together in dialogue, they each bring their own perspectives and histories. Fusing horizons does not require turning these differences into sameness; quite the contrary, it clarifies the dialogue that occurs between what is familiar and what is unfamiliar and makes it clear that there is never a complete understanding. Thus, interpretation is central to approaching knowledge, and each person's interpretation is different (Warnke 1987). The emphasis in our course hermeneutically was on understanding and interpreting concepts while building upon personal situatedness. Phenomenology layers well with hermeneutics as it supports trying to arrive at a description of phenomena; 'from a phenomenological point of view, to do research is always to question the way we experience the world, to want to know the world in which we live as human beings' (van Manen 1990, 5). This approach does not look at a problem *per se*, or for a solution – it looks at an experience and tries to see things through others' points of view. Thus, a hermeneutic phenomenological approach provided a way of capturing different ways of knowing and understanding, as it provided insight into the essence of experiences for ourselves and for each other. As we consider how relationships manifested themselves within the context of this study and how we worked to deconstruct and then reconstruct the roles of 'teacher' and 'student', we next summarize the structures of the course to contextualize the discussion that follows.

The course

This photo (Figure 1) shows a typical cogenerative dialogue from our course. There are eight people around a table, though not all are visible. The table was created by participants each session, as the classroom actually had individual desks. Before each meeting, people moved the desks so that we could sit together. Participants did not select 'set' seats and simply sat around the table in different spots each week. In this photo, Beth is at the top of the table and she was sharing with the group the details of an interaction with a child during the previous science lesson and there is evidence of the typical focus of the group on whoever was speaking at a given moment.

Many of our cogenerative dialogues[3] focused on the lessons we were coteaching in the elementary classroom, and a central focus was discussing what happened in the previous week (from our varied perspectives) and using these experiences to construct the upcoming science lessons.

Figure 1. Listening to one another.

Cogenerative dialogues were central, as they provided a space for revealing differing perspectives, experiences, and opinions. Importantly, a key motive within cogenerative dialogues is to: 'enact forms of culture that expand the agency of all participants and produce agreements on how to enact curricula differently in a classroom so as to afford improvements in the quality of teaching and learning' (Tobin and Roth 2006, 88). Combined with cogenerative dialogues, coteaching served as a central approach to learning how to teach, and coresearching mediated learning how to research one's practice. As a whole, this approach provided polysemic perspectives in our teaching and research.

> **Chris:** It is important for me as an instructor of a course to not only say that I value people's input, but to be ready to accept their suggestions – even if perhaps it is not what I might have tried to do in the classroom. This can be difficult sometimes, as there are often my 'favorite' activities. But it is crucial that I open myself up to the suggestions of others, even if it means not being able to implement activities that I might consider to be the 'best' activity at that moment.

The context

Our course[4] met twice weekly over 15 weeks, once each week on the college campus and once at a local elementary school. There were seven pre-service teacher participants: three were juniors and four were seniors. Chris was the instructor of the course and had been a faculty member at the college for four years. Chris's background includes having taught elementary science and at the time of the study she was beginning her third year as a doctoral student. The elementary school is a K-5 school with approximately 500 children enrolled in the year of our collaboration. The college is a small private college located about 30 minutes outside a major metropolitan area in the northeastern USA. There were fewer than 2000 undergraduate students in the college as a whole, and the undergraduate teacher preparation program consisted of approximately 65 students enrolled in the childhood education program (leading to state certification for first through sixth grade).

The research process

This research is part of a larger study on the role of collaborative field-based science methods courses, which documents and analyzes six semester-long courses. In this paper, we write about the fall 2007 semester, in which all cogenerative dialogues and cotaught lessons were videotaped, and these served as the central data source for this study. Our joint analyses began after the course concluded, as Chris invited participants to join a research group that met bi-weekly for the following semester. All members of the course during fall 2007 participated in research afterwards to varying degrees, depending on their time and interest, and numerous collaborative papers and presentations have emerged from this study (e.g., Siry and Lowell, forthcoming). As a critical ethnography (Carspecken 1996), the research project was a lens to examine the forces acting upon teachers and students and to consider issues of power and authority as manifested in educational institutions (McLaren 2007).

Beth and two other pre-service teachers chose to participate in a weekly research group, and our initial analyses consisted of discussing within this group our recollections of course events. From these discussions, we decided to view videos individually and then discuss them in research meetings. Overall, our analytic interpretative process was quite messy, as structures emerged and shifted with our needs. For this particular paper, we drew on autoethnographic and co/autoethnographic methods to frame our analysis (Coia and Taylor 2009). These analyses led to an initial focus on the ways of collaboration, and the focus on working together structured our individual and collective experiences in the course. As we began to conceptualize this paper specifically, we considered the broad question of: *What did the structure of collaborative practices enable in the context of a field-based methods course?* In holding this initial question, we then narrowed our focus to specific ways this structure revealed and supported a methodological stance towards working together around and against hierarchies and how this in turn supported pre-service teachers in understanding the multilogical, polysemic ways we each make sense of our own experiences as we work with others.

Working 'with'...

Next, we examine three different findings related to engaging in collaborative practices in the context of our course and research, as this approach has: (1) mediated our learning about teaching as a collective endeavor; (2) highlighted the importance and differences in individual experiences; and (3) supported us in reconsidering and reconstructing the role of teacher. We discuss these findings in this section and surround them in meaning with examples and discussions relative to the implications of working 'with'.

Working 'with'... to learn about teaching as a collective endeavor

Grounded in sociocultural theory, we consider teaching and learning as culture (Sewell 1999). As such, we conceive of knowledge as socially constructed and thus enacted. Cogenerative dialogues supported the co-construction and enactment of knowledge as they provided an opportunity to revisit classroom events. Reflexive knowledge production was ongoing, as we met to plan teaching activities, discuss events that occurred in the elementary classroom, and share successes, challenges, and new ideas. The following excerpt[5] is of an interaction between Olga, Kate, Barb,

Eileen and Chris as they share, debate, and build upon previous experiences in planning an upcoming activity originally planned to incorporate children's written reflections on their science lessons:

> Olga: I think that if we have the kids write their thoughts down, it will take too long. They are re:ally slow writers.
> Kate: What if the data sheets we develop have some writing though, and that each table of kids work together to generate a sentence that sums up their idea, and then <u>all</u> the kids at that table can write that sentence.
> Barb: Or, we could build on that idea and then also have a sentence with a <u>blank</u> at the end that they fill in, like it would sa:y, my favorite part of this science activity wa::s, and have a blank space.
> Eileen: I don't know about that idea-
> Barb: Well, then they can think back together on the activity and think of their <u>own</u> words that are what they liked.

After three minutes of discussion of a similar activity Barb had seen in a classroom observation, they return to the idea of worksheets for their lesson, and the interaction continues with the following exchange:

> Krista: Maybe it won't take <u>too</u> long if we ask them to do this as part of our lessons and we can just do [it]
> Kate: [Do] we have to get it done? Can't we just have it as a choice and then if we get to it we get to it?-
> Barb: Maybe we could suggest to Mrs. Nevins that she have a science journal? She has to teach so::: much writing, she could have them write about what they did with us in their journal, then we can focus on the science. If she incorporates it into her language time, then <u>we</u> can have them just write those individual words and we combine everything.
> Chris: Well, if many of our lessons will use a weekly data sheet for organizing our activities, this idea of connecting it with their existing journals might work really well — should we suggest it to her and see what she says?

This interaction began with Olga expressing her hesitation that too much of their (very limited) time in the classroom would be taken up by the students writing their reflections on the activity. In response to her comment, two possible ways to incorporate a summarized approach to writing are introduced, as Kate suggests the groups of children decide on one sentence, and Barb counters that there could be a blank space for children to complete individually. Eileen is clearly skeptical as she states, 'I don't know about that idea', to which Barb clarifies her justification of the fill-in-the-blank idea as something that would allow the students to contribute their own ideas to the worksheets. These pre-service teachers had taught only one other lesson together, which was the first lesson most of them had ever taught. As the conversation unfolded, Barb introduced an activity she had seen in another classroom, and she brought these experiences to the group with an exchange that lasted over three minutes, concerning her observations similar to her suggestion. In refocusing to the activity they were trying to develop, Krista suggests having the students write quickly, but Kate interjects her thoughts on having the sheet as an option ('Can't we just have it as a choice and then if we get to it we get to it?'). As the exchange concludes, Chris reminds the group that they had decided previously to use weekly data sheets and thus having the writing as a choice would connect with the structure they already planned, and she turns to a consideration of the classroom teacher with, 'should we suggest it to her and see what she says?'

It is critical to provide opportunity for dialogue to open up the space to reveal different perspectives on teaching and learning. For us, cogenerative dialogues and coteaching provided the structures to do this, as they served as a method and a methodology for moving towards a multiplicity of perspectives in the collective construction of the course.

Through the structure of shared responsibility, we have pushed back on the traditional notion of the classroom as a place of individual successes and instead have created an environment where collaboration is central to working towards the success of each and everyone involved. Collaboration can paint a

> **Beth:** Coteaching allowed us to feel supported not only by Chris, as the professor, like maybe in a traditional student-teaching approach to a lesson, but as much by our peers as well. The attitude while we were teaching was more of a 'one for all, and all for one' sentiment, because of the investment we have all made in the lessons and the relationships we formed through the constant dialogues we had.

clearer picture of multiple meanings, as collective organization and creation of thoughts can be a transformative experience for participants. Lander and English situate their perspective on collaboration as 'relational and responsive knowledge' (2000, 348), and in this perspective they draw on Mikhail Bakhtin's (1984, 110) conception of truth: 'Truth is not to be found inside the head of an individual person, it is born between people collectively searching for truth, in the process of their dialogic interaction.' In collectively searching for 'truth' in the way that Bakhtin framed it, working 'with' takes an endless path, as we envision the possibilities of working with: thinking with, talking with, teaching with, learning with, empathizing with, crying with, laughing with ...

Working 'with'... to highlight the phenomenological, individual experience

At times, our dialogues revealed moments that we saw really differently from our situated perspectives, and this highlighted the need for different voices and points of view. The following exchange is from an encounter in which Beth and Eileen discuss their two very different interactions during the same lesson:

> Beth: I feel like, at least the kids at m:y table, didn't really know what to DO at the tables. I feel like the explanations we give need to make sure that they are clear, so that they know what they need to do before they leave the rug, because once they get to the tables [with the science activities] it is IMPOSSIBLE to stop them to tell them what they are expected to try to do. I mean, I was the ONLY one at that table, so I had to really walk around and make sure they understood what to do, which was fi::ne, but they started really confused, and I don't know if it was because of the transition where they had to first start at the rug and then go to the table? Somehow it all got lost-
>
> Chris: That's interesting, it also was something very new too, which they hadn't done before, so that could have contributed, did anyone else find that at their tables?

Eileen: Well, I had something a bit different as I had ONE kid who really didn't know what to draw, so I said, well, maybe draw that <u>frog</u>, because he was talking about frogs and butterflies, so he drew a frog.
Chris: OK, so how did that work out?
Eileen: He was <u>unfocused</u> though, he kept looking around, and trying to think of what to draw.
Kaylie: That doesn't mean he was <u>unfocused</u>, remember that there were a lot of us there, and that can be exciting too.

This episode presents an example in which two people clearly had quite different experiences in the same classroom. Beth begins by explaining her position that the children needed clear explanations in discussions (which occurred 'on the rug') before they moved to tables. As she explains in a frustrated tone that the children began confused ('somehow it all got lost'), Eileen responds by sharing that her dilemma was quite different, as with raised eyebrows she shakes her head from side to side and says, 'I had one kid who really didn't know what to draw'. She continues to state her thoughts that the child was not focused on the activity ('he was unfocused though, he kept looking around, and trying to think of what to draw').

> **Chris:** I have learned from teaching this course that we are often surprised by the differences in our interpretations and experiences in the same elementary classroom. We spend a lot of time planning lessons together that we think will go 'well', and discover that things rarely go as planned, as children interact with our activities in many different ways. Having weekly dialogues with an explicit purpose of improving our teaching provides an ongoing structure to emphasize the complexity of teaching.

Alfred Schutz (1967) discussed the importance of other-awareness (Fremdverstehen), which we position as a critical methodological consideration for teaching and research. He wrote that knowledge is on the inside and on the outside, and thus the only way to know about the 'inside' is to ask the other person. Part of our focus on collaborative structures provided a space to talk out individual thoughts and experiences, especially as related to learning about children. This other-awareness emphasizes the importance of working with others to explore their understandings. We cannot know whether or not the child was unfocused, but clearly his reaction surprised Eileen, and this opened the conversation to discussing possibilities.

Recognizing students' different reactions emphasizes the value of turning to colleagues and sharing perspectives, and listening to/learning from each other's experiences and concerns. Christa Albrecht-Crane has argued that the process of becoming teachers should involve creating new ways of relating to one another. She writes that teachers should

> **Beth:** I see that I evolved in respect to being understanding and accepting of others' opinions. With good communication and the understanding that everyone has differing, valid opinions, it is possible to find middle ground, to agree, or to agree to disagree.

not focus on discovering 'the truth in one's teaching, but rather to use one's teaching to arrive at a multiplicity of truth-making relationships' (2005, 492).

The conversation in this encounter continued, with Kaylie discussing the possibility that the boy was simply distracted by us as extra adults in the classroom, as she immediately responds with, 'that doesn't mean he was unfocused' while leaning into the table, shaking her head from side to side. She emphasizes her point by adding that, 'there were a lot of us there, and that can be exciting too'.

Coming together across a variety of perspectives and positions requires being open to ideas different from our own. Joe Kincheloe advocated radical listening, that is, listening to another person or reading another person's work with the explicit purpose of trying to understand their perspectives and working to understand 'their standpoints and axiological commitments' (Tobin 2009, 505). As we made explicit the dimensions of difference between us, we stressed the need to listen and the need to empathize, and we focused on how this was manifested within the field-based course and within the production of knowledge through our collaborative research. We opened ourselves up to others' perspectives and tried to listen to experiences that were perhaps different than our own (while trying to avoid imposing our own perspectives on these).

Working 'with'... to reconstruct the role of a teacher

Traditionally we see that teachers are expected to 'know' and learners are expected 'not to know'; in our experiences, this has been the case in pre-service teacher education as well, with the professor often positioned as the person with the knowledge to provide. In contrast, we found that in cogenerating understandings through dialogues and collaboration, the knowledge was co-created by course participants. The following interaction occurred mid-way through the semester, as we discussed our experiences together thus far. The conversation began with the resistance participants had initially felt towards the unfamiliar concept of co-constructing their own learning and teaching experiences (as Beth alludes to in the opening vignette). Chris asks the group to consider their initial resistance within the educational structures they had experienced as students thus far, and the conversation turns to contrasting previous experiences with their encounters within the collaborative course:

```
Beth:   I feel like you see us being on the same plane as you,
        where in other courses, the teacher, the professors, they
        talk down [and]
Kate:   [It's] very much they're the teachers and we are the
        students
Beth:   Yeah. Even though WE are supposed to not do that in our
        classroom, like with the kids, we are supposed to make
        them feel like it is our classroom together, yet a lot of
        our education professors make it their class,
Chris:  How do you mean?
Beth:   Well, if you don't do their work, the way they want it,
        to this specific way, then you get a bad grade.
Chris:  But there is a million different ways to do it right-
Beth:   Well, exactly, that's what I mean, and that's what we are
        supposed to learn as teachers, but the others don't seem
        to see it that way.
```

Beth and Kate explain their thoughts on professors in other courses as the ones who control the knowledge. They refer to their positionings as students, and the higher positioning of professors, with their comments 'they talk down' and 'they're the teachers and we are the students'. Granted, in the institutional structures of a college course, certainly they are in the role of 'students', however, their point in this interaction is greater than role. It correlates to their future roles as teachers, as Beth points out with her comment that 'Even though we are supposed to not do that in our classroom, like with the kids'.

We see this sense of 'being on the same plane' between the group as something that was mediated by our explicit focus on collaborative structures. This evolved over time, as our relationships shifted through the complex combination of ongoing dialogue, open-ended activities, flexible expectations, and sharing of responsibility for teaching the children. The course structure of weekly dialogues provided a space to ask important questions – how are structures and roles within them set up to perpetuate power? Why is teacher education structured the way it is? How can we correlate our own learning within our course with how we can collaborate with, and cogenerate knowledge with, our future students and colleagues?

Beth: Chris expected that our ideas, observations, and difficulties were shared as pieces of the learning. What we had to say was important to her. The structure allowed for us to become a group of teachers working together and the lines dividing her as teacher from us as students disappeared. I believe this is what it all comes down to. It was never about her 'agenda'. It was always about us, and what we needed to succeed in teaching science, so that the curriculum came from us, instead of making us come to the curriculum.

Who controls the knowledge? What do we do about prescribed curricula and standards? Key to approaching these questions is deconstructing the role of teacher and the role of student. However, deconstructing is not enough, as the critical element is how we *reconstruct* these roles. 'Transformative intellectuals need to develop a discourse that unites the language of critique with the language of possibility, so that social educators recognize that they can make changes' (Giroux 2004, 211). In this process of reconstructing the roles of teacher and student, we generated local theory about teaching and learning with the overt purpose of drawing connections to our practices as educators. The questions we asked have

Chris: As we deconstructed the deeply embedded notions of teacher and student and worked with collaborative pedagogies and research methodologies, my students became positioned as more than simply 'subjects' of my research, and I have both sought to inform the research with their perspectives and also sought to share their perspectives with others.

shed light on the possibilities for the participants as future teachers to be able to work within, around, and across existing structures. Being open to other possibilities mediates making changes and expanding roles, and we hope this extends to their schools.

Returning to the complexities of co-

To draw all of the discussions in this paper together, we return to the notion of collaboration and highlight certain themes running through our experiences and, thus, through this paper as one set of representations of these experiences. As members of the group negotiated the structure of the course and their teaching experiences, they needed to be open to embracing multi-logicality (Kincheloe 2008) and acknowledge that there are multiple realities and different ways of interpreting events in one's lifeworld. As we worked towards multi-logicality and an epistemology of plurality, one that both seeks and *requires* a multitude of perspectives, a key question to consider is: why is this relevant in teacher education specifically?

Through this process, we connected to future roles as elementary teachers and how groundings in complex methodologies can carry through to views on classroom teaching and learning with their future students. Participants became positioned as knowledge producers, rather than as consumers of a hegemonic truth. An important consideration for a science methods course specifically is that the co-construction of activities challenged the notion that there is one right method for teaching science. In addition to the vignettes presented herein to illustrate ways participants perceived an activity, there were myriad similar interactions in which the purposes and outcomes of science were discussed, debated, and made sense of.

> **Beth:** When Chris initially said she wanted us to share what we were thinking about our lessons, I automatically associated this with telling her what I thought she wanted to hear. We expected that to be her job as the professor. However, only a few weeks later we were all involved in a discussion about Krista's lesson which is presented above. We are all posing questions, providing suggestions, and critically analyzing the ideas in regards to what we had seen in the classroom so far. We were no longer students waiting for a professor to tell us what to do or how to look at a lesson; Instead, we were teachers and collaborators, providing advice to Krista based on what we each knew about elementary teaching.

Conducting research that expands roles and contests hierarchies

Cowriting and coresearching contest the traditional epistemological/ontological hierarchies that position researcher above researched, and in sharing research we not only expand our roles but also work to push back against the 'cult of the expert' (Kincheloe 2003). We do not want the purpose of research to be only the production of theory isolated from practice. Indeed, it is the improvement of practice that is of utmost importance to us, and this is the purpose for us in examining and interpreting experiences through collaboratively researching.

> **Chris:** In researching pre-service teacher education, a primary concern is improving the practice of all participants. I continually have asked myself: how am I helping to produce useful knowledge, and who is this knowledge useful for?

Inherent in structuring ways of working *with* is a focus on seeking to achieve a polysemic understanding. Polyphonic methods are a necessity as we attempt to represent what happened in a given situation. However, it is not enough to have multiple voices, as they could all be saying the same thing. Thus, this research has emerged through a theoretical stance that dialogue is required to work towards polysemia, as in the shared creation of text representing differing perspectives and understandings we push the boundaries of what it means to do research. Knowing that we all bring our own experiences, expectations, and contexts to a situation (and thus we each see the same moments differently), it becomes imperative to seek to illuminate the meaning we give to moments that might initially seem the same.

We link our experiences and expectations that have grown from coteaching and coresearching with embracing complexity and notions of difference. We needed to turn back upon our experiences to reflexively become aware of our different perspectives, and in that process, we evolved in our understandings of our experiences and of ourselves. 'When you and I are immediately involved with each other, every experience is colored by that involvement' (Schutz 1967, 167). We contend that the process of becoming aware is one that can be open and dialogic, as we learned to embrace the realities of social life that remind us that everyone experiences the world differently.

Central to this is power in all its forms, and we considered dominant forms of power and how they shape our experiences. As we discussed the power that we are aware of, we tried to reveal power structures that we might be unaware of. We also sought to recognize the power structures that are inherent in what we do – for example, ultimately, Chris had to give grades and meet the objectives of the course set by the college, and the participants needed to complete the course and ideally be positioned to pass teacher certification exams. However, how we go about this does not have to be top-down and hierarchical, and together we discussed possibilities for grading, as participants developed assignments that met objectives set by the college and met their own needs. In this way, multiple options for completing course expectations emerged from the group. Within collaborative structures that included such explicit conversations, we worked to reveal and analyze how power shapes what we do as teachers and as learners within institutions.

Such collective approaches to teaching, learning, and researching together can support a reciprocity within what we do, and such reciprocity 'implies give and take, a mutual negotiation of meaning and power' (Lather 1991, 57). It is this give-and-take that is carefully negotiated along with the negotiating of co-constructed meanings of teaching and learning. Our main focus has been examining the purposes of education and educational research (as we see it), and positioning coteaching/cowriting/coresearching as ways to co-construct experiences in the academy to the benefit of all participants in teaching and research (and, of course, our students). Doing this within teacher education required dialogue focused on connections between our current roles as teacher and students and the participants' future roles as teachers. Tricia Kress (this issue) calls for 'stepping out of the academic brew' (267) to focus on the authority we bring as teachers and critique this authority in order to work to purposefully break it down. In the process of transforming together the structures of our course, we worked to heed Kress's call to flatten knowledge hierarchies.

Where do we go from here?

Reflecting on our experiences, teaching and researching together has led us to recognize a struggle with what comes next, and we ask of each other: *What happens after we leave these situations?* Collectively we learned to teach science, as we learned about teaching, and learned about each other. Participants exhibited increased agency in a wide variety of situations, and we felt able to take (and share) responsibility for teaching and learning. Yet the reality is that there have been moments outside of our course in which participants found themselves no longer positioned as producers of knowledge in the same vein. The following is an excerpt from written conversation in the genre of metalogue that guided the creation of this paper. The use of metalogue can constitute an approach to collective remembering (Roth and Tobin 2004). We use this excerpt to illustrate the conceptualizations and conversations that emerged through the process of producing knowledge together, particularly as we explored our struggle with what comes next:

Beth: After being in such a collaborative setting as the science methods course with you [Chris], and making such a personal transformation in seeing how beneficial working together can be, I have had difficulties in working with others who do not wish to share responsibility in the classroom, both in the college classroom and the elementary classroom. After taking your class I moved on to another semester of undergraduate classes that fit the traditional method of teacher-directed. I had to 'bite my tongue' and stop myself from raising my hand after realizing my attempts to share information would fall on deaf ears, both from the professor and the other students. Recently in a class where we were required to work with elementary school students in a group, a peer said to me, 'Why do we have to do this? Didn't we already have to work with a student for another course? I just want to get this class over with.' As I listened to her share her opinion, I couldn't help but think that other people must feel this way too.

Chris: These are good points that you bring up Beth, and we have spoken during the past years a bit about how your development through our course has also caused some dilemmas for you – in that you aren't always in the role that you *can* share responsibility – that is really important to talk about openly. I'm thinking about this idea that I have been struggling with relative to working with people who don't see the need for collaboration and trying to share responsibilities the way that I do. I believe really it is okay for different people to experience a moment in different ways, in fact, I think that is probably how every moment is at every time. However, what do we do in situations when the difference is that the others aren't comfortable with the idea of polysemicity and are looking for sameness?

Beth: Recently I have also been in situations where co-workers will not share responsibilities within the classroom, either giving away or taking all of it. Communication is difficult with other professionals who see teaching as a solo activity, especially when you think of it as collaborative. After experiencing firsthand the benefits of collaboration it is difficult to understand why others don't try to work with their colleagues more often. However, it highlights an opportunity for me to be open to them, and show them what they are missing out on, if they are perhaps willing to try to work together a little at a time.

As we work to change the structures that we can change, we recognize those that are harder to change, and it is precisely these that we keep in our collective focus moving forward. 'Authority' is an important consideration for pre-service teachers in particular, as issues of classroom management and administrative structures are generally paramount concerns as they begin to frame themselves as teachers. Ira Shor and Paulo Freire (1987) wrote on the possibilities for liberatory pedagogies to transform education, and they drew a distinction between authority and authoritarianism. We have discovered together that while authority in classrooms might be unavoidable, we ought to be 'open to sharing it and having the students emerge as co-directors of the curriculum' (Shor and Freire 1987, 91). Recognizing authority within a given structure does not need to be authoritative, and our dialogical structure has supported the breakdown of authoritarianistic approaches as we worked together towards transformation within ourselves as teachers and learners.

The dilemma still remains of what to do when those around us do not share our desire for breaking down hierarchical structures. In fact, as Beth mentions in her last textbox, she was not initially invested in this notion either. The questions remain for us: How do we deal with those who seek sameness? What do we do when those whom we are 'with' don't want to share responsibilities or collaborate? As we consider these questions, we wonder if it is perhaps in continually 'walking the walk' as we remain open to difference that we can persist at breaking down the hierarchies that exist and ideally allow and encourage others to join us in the process.

The paradox of documenting research

This paper attempts to weave a narrative perspective of our experiences within and around a collaborative field-based science methods course. It is not intended to present the 'truth', as there are many truths, and we envision that we could write a very different paper if two different participants from the same course constructed it. We recognize that this presents a paradox, given that there is no complete truth on the one hand, yet on the other hand we try within research to present something as close to authentic to the moment as possible (Hølge-Hazelton and Krøjer 2008), and we stress that what we present herein is our individual and shared sense-making around the possibilities in working in collaboration.

Implications for practice and moving forward

We have generated perspectives relevant for what we do in our future teaching through considering the complexities of the collaborations we experienced. As we have come to ways of knowing constructed together, around a shared purpose of teaching and learning to teach science, we recognize that what is 'known' and experienced is inherently different from person to person. There are implications of this work for teacher education programs, as it emphasizes the importance of establishing a focus in teacher education on learning how to teach through holistic, 'real-world' experiences, coupled with substantial opportunities for reflection, discussion, and action. While there are certainly many teacher education programs with practica or other types of field-based experiences, it is not the norm that pre-service teachers and faculty share these. Emphasizing such an approach requires a shift in the focus of field experiences to being in classrooms together with a focus on reflexive experiences and generating dialogic understandings.

Our initial research question was: What did the structure of collaborative practices enable in the context of a field-based methods course? As we examined different ways we worked with each other, our analyses led us to frame the ways we came to hold (often shared) meanings around our differences in three distinct ways: we learned about teaching as a collective endeavor, highlighted individual experiences, and reconsidered and reconstructed the role of teacher. Though we have pulled them apart here for the sake of interpretation and discussion, these emphases are interwoven, and ultimately layer together to support us as we focus on conducting research that expands roles and contests hierarchies.

We have explored herein some of the ways in which we worked with each other and we see a wide variety of opportunities for working 'with'; theorizing with, researching with, talking with, writing with, being with, thinking with... In doing so, our examination of relationships between individuals and the collective has been framed by our taking apart and examining the roles of 'teacher' and 'student' with the purpose of reconstructing these in ways that are not predicated on authoritative constructions, as we examined some meanings of 'working with'. For us, this research has served to emphasize the importance of acknowledging that we are not ever standing alone (as a teacher or student) when we are in a classroom:

> **Beth:** It is powerful to see your peers as teachers and as learners; I hope that I can support my future students in sharing responsibility and learning from each other.

Acknowledgements

We are grateful to Tricia Kress for inviting us to submit to this special issue of the *International Journal of Qualitative Studies in Education*, and to Carolyne Ali-Khan and two anonymous reviewers who provided critical feedback and suggestions to this work.

Notes

1. The use of > emerged from discussions with Carolyne Ali-Khan. We gratefully acknowledge her contribution and support of this work.
2. For a comprehensive discussion of coteaching and of cogenerative dialogues, please see the following review chapters: Bayne (2009) and Martin (2009).
3. Coteaching and cogenerative dialogue for us are interwoven and inseparable, yet for the purpose of discussion and analysis we draw them apart here.
4. The specific structure and unfolding of one semester of such a course are described in Siry (forthcoming).
5. Transcript notations were adapted from Roth (2006) who cites Gail Jefferson (e.g., 1989) as his source. The following conventions were used:

really	Underline indicates emphasis or stress in delivery
ALL	Capital letters are used when an utterance is louder than the surrounding talk
idea-	The hyphen mark indicates a sudden stop.
wa::s	Each colon indicates approximately a 0.1 second lengthening of sounds longer than normal
done?	Punctuation marks are used as characteristics of speech rather than grammar features
just do [it]	Square brackets indicate overlapping speech

References

Albrecht-Crane, C. 2005. Pedagogy as friendship: Identity and affect in the conservative classroom. *Cultural Studies* 19, no. 4: 491–514.

Ares, N. 2008. Appropriating roles and relations of power in collaborative learning. *International Journal of Qualitative Studies in Education* 21, no. 2: 99–121.

Ashenfelter, J.W., and R.K. Hanson. 1971. A teaching laboratory for a methods course: Rationale, description, and evaluation. *Journal of Teacher Education* 22, no. 2: 189–93.

Bakhtin, M. 1984. *Problems of Dostoevsky's poetics*. Ed. and trans. C. Emerson. Minneapolis, MN: University of Minnesota Press.

Bayne, G.U. 2009. Cogenerative dialogues: The creation of interstitial culture in the New York metropolis. In *World of science education: Handbook of research in North America*, ed. W.-M. Roth and K. Tobin, 513–28. Rotterdam: Sense Publishing.

Carspecken, P.F. 1996. *Critical ethnography in educational research*. New York: Routledge.

Coia, L., and M. Taylor. 2009. Co/autoethnography: Exploring our teaching selves collaboratively. In *Research methods for the self-study of practice,* ed. D.L. Tidwell, M.L. Heston, and L.M. Fitzgerald, 3–16. Dordrecht: Springer.

Drumheller, S.J., and J. Paris. 1966. An effective approach for incorporating teaching experiences in methods courses. *Journal of Teacher Education* 17, no. 3: 290–5.

Elmesky, R., and T. Tobin. 2005. Expanding our understandings of urban science education by expanding the roles of students as researchers. *Journal of Research in Science Teaching* 42, no. 7: 807–28.

Gadamer, H.-G. 2004. *Truth and method.* London: Continuum.

Giroux, H. 2004. Teachers as transformative intellectuals. In *Educational foundations: An anthology of critical readings,* ed. A.S. Canestrari and B.A. Marlowe, 205–12. Thousand Oaks, CA: Sage.

Greene, M. 1995. *Releasing the imagination: Essays on education, the arts, and social change.* San Francisco, CA: Jossey-Bass.

Hølge-Hazelton, B., and J. Krøjer. 2008. (Re)constructing strategies: A methodological experiment on representation. *International Journal of Qualitative Studies in Education* 21, no. 1: 19–25.

Kincheloe, J. 2003. *Teachers as researchers: Qualitative inquiry as a path to empowerment.* 2nd ed. New York: RoutledgeFalmer.

Kincheloe, J. 2008. *Critical pedagogy primer.* New York: Peter Lang.

Kress, T. 2011. Stepping out of the academic brew: Using critical research to break down hierarchies of knowledge production. *International Journal of Qualitative Studies in Education* 24, no. 3: 267–83.

Lander, D.A., and L.M. English. 2000. Doing research 'with': Reading and writing our difference. *Reflective Practice* 1, no. 3: 343–56.

Lather, P. 1991. *Getting smart: Feminist research and pedagogy with/in the postmodern.* New York: Routledge.

Martin, S. 2005. The social and cultural dimension of successful teaching and learning of science in an urban high school. Doctoral diss., Curtin University of Technology, Australia.

Martin, S. 2009. Learning to teach science. In *World of science education: Handbook of research in North America*, ed. W-R. Roth and K. Tobin, 567–86. Rotterdam: Sense Publishers.

Martin, S.N., and K. Scantlebury. 2009. More than a conversation: Using cogenerative dialogues in the professional development of high school chemistry teachers. *Educational Assessment, Evaluation, and Accountability* 21, no. 2: 119–36.

McLaren, P. 2007. *Life in schools: An introduction to critical pedagogy in the foundations of education.* 5th ed. Boston, MA: Pearson Education.

Roth, W.-M. 2006. Conversation analysis: Deconstructing social relations in the making. In *Doing educational research: A handbook,* ed. K. Tobin and J. Kincheloe, 235–67. Rotterdam: Sense Publishers.

Roth, W.-M., and K. Tobin. 2004. Co-generative dialoguing and metaloguing: Reflexivity of processes and genres. *Forum Qualitative Sozialforschung* [Forum: Qualitative Social Research] [on-line journal] 5, no. 3. http://www.qualitative-research.net/index.php/fqs/article/view/560 (accessed November 12, 2010).

Schutz, A. 1967. *The phenomenology of the social world.* Evanston, IL: Northwestern University Press.

Sewell, W.H. 1999. The concept(s) of culture. In *Beyond the cultural turn: New directions in the study of society and culture,* ed. V.E. Bonnell and L. Hunt, 35–61. Berkeley, CA: University of California Press.

Shor, I., and P. Freire. 1987. *A pedagogy for liberation: Dialogues on transforming education.* Granby, MA: Bergin and Garvey Publishers.

Siry, C. 2009. Fostering solidarity and transforming identities: A collaborative approach to elementary science teacher education. Doctoral diss., The Graduate Center, City University of New York.

Siry, C. Forthcoming. Emphasizing collaborative practices in learning to teach: Coteaching and cogenerative dialogue in a field-based methods course. *Teaching Education.*

Siry C., and C. Ali-Khan. Forthcoming. Writing we: Collaborative text in educational research. In *Critical pedagogy in the 21st century*, ed. C. Malott and B. Portfilio. Charlotte, NC: Information Age Publishing.

Siry, C., and N. Lowell. Forthcoming. Exploring the complexities of learning to teach: Collaborative methods and participatory structures in teacher education. In *Producing successful science and mathematics education: Urban teachers and students working collaboratively*, ed. K. Tobin and A. Shady. Rotterdam: Sense Publishers.

Siry, C., and S. Martin, with S. Baker, N. Lowell, J. Marvin, and Y. Wilson. 2010. Coteaching in science education courses: Transforming teacher education through shared responsibility. In *Coteaching in international contexts: Research and practice*, ed. C. Murphy and K. Scantlebury, 57–78. Rotterdam: Springer Press.

Sleeter, C. 2008. Equity, democracy, and neoliberal assaults on teacher education. *Teaching and Teacher Education* 24, no. 8: 1947–57.

ten Dam, G.T., and S. Blom. 2006. Learning through participation. The potential of school-based teacher education for developing a professional identity. *Teaching and Teacher Education* 22, no. 6: 647–60.

Tobin, K. 2009. Tuning into others' voices: Radical listening, learning from difference, and escaping oppression. *Cultural Studies of Science Education* 4, no. 3: 505–11.

Tobin, K., and W.-M. Roth. 2006. *Teaching to learn: A view from the field*. Rotterdam: Sense Publishers.

van Manen, M. 1990. *Researching lived experience: Human science for an action sensitive pedagogy*. Albany, NY: SUNY Press.

Warnke, G. 1987. *Gadamer: Hermeneutics, tradition and reason*. Palo Alto, CA: Stanford University Press.

Keeping a 'vigilant critique': unpacking critical praxis as teacher educators

Patricia Paugh[a] and Elizabeth Robinson[b]

[a]Department of Curriculum and Instruction, University of Massachusetts Boston, 100 Morrissey Boulevard, Boston, MA 02125, USA; [b]Department of Teacher Education and Curriculum Studies (TECS), University of Massachusetts Amherst, 813 North Pleasant Street, Amherst, MA 01003, USA

> The practice of a critical pedagogy was the impetus for our involvement in an urban in-district master's program with a mission that included developing a 'critical praxis' for all participants. Early on we were challenged to rethink our stance as 'critical educators' when teachers resisted what we intended to be 'empowering' course practices, assigning readings written by teacher researchers. This resistance required us to question whether our pedagogy was honoring their experiences as well as inviting the collaborative generation of knowledge that we professed to encourage. Drawing our methodology from Freire's notion of 'generative words' and Bakhtin's notion of 'writing the self into the text', we analyzed artifacts collected from our teaching over several cycles using critical discourse analysis. Our analysis reminds us to remain 'vigilant'. That is, not to ignore difference but to look carefully for often hidden opportunities offered for deeper learning when multiple perspectives come into contact.

The advent of 'No Child Left Behind (NCLB)' legislation and 'Reading First' funding was accompanied by an all-out media attack on US urban schools and urban teachers in particular. The stated purpose of the NCLB Act of 2002 is to help all students to reach proficiency in English language arts/reading and mathematics by the year 2014. Through the Reading First Initiative of NCLB, reading instruction and assessment have been dramatically impacted by legislation requiring a single and narrow view of the reading process and high-stake exams to assess students' progress and penalize schools not making adequate yearly progress. The school district where we (authors Pat and Elizabeth) were initiating an in-district master's program was struggling to meet NCLB and Reading First mandates and was a focal point for negative media coverage. 'Flawed instruction seen at state's failing schools' was a headline in the major state newspaper, drawing not only local, but state attention to this high-poverty, highly segregated urban school district. As we began teaching our first course, *Practitioner Research,* we asked the teachers (several who worked in a school that had been vilified in local and state news publications) to write responses that outlined their own experiences and perspectives. Dyan,[1] a White English dominant teacher working as a special educator, wrote:

> The one article mentioned that our school was chaos, which is a lie, and that our principal was not available for comments which is another lie ... [in actuality we were] quickly thrown into turmoil [during the state evaluation process] ... between the school department, state, and the school it was a nightmare. We were one of the first schools to be identified as underperforming and we were one of the first schools to go through this agonizing process. There was no one at the School Department who knew exactly what the state was looking for, and there was definitely a power struggle within the administration and the school department ... We later found out that not one member of the panel had been assigned or had worked in city schools.

However, Carmen, a Latina English as a second language (ESL) teacher, while recognizing the negativity, took the blame to heart more readily:

> 'Flawed instruction seen at state's failing schools' is a very negative article against teachers and principals. I believe that there must be a few teachers and administrators who still aren't on the right teaching track, but I don't think this is what is causing schools to fail. I truly believe that No Child Left Behind, [state test] assessments, and the newly passed state law, question #2 [English Only Law], have changed teaching and teaching expectations all around. Since these changes, the state and administrators expect all students to pass assessments and to be proficient. I think this is a process, and is going to take some time. If teachers continue to be trained and monitored, eventually our way of thinking and our teaching skills will get better.

For Carmen, the negative publicity produced its intended effect. As a teacher receiving blame, Carmen positioned herself to 'try harder' and improve her skills to meet what Dyan noted was an unclear set of expectations imposed by powerful forces who had little experience with students in urban schools.

Adopting a 'critical stance' as teacher educators

Our master's program was designed to support teachers in this environment by developing solid language and literacy knowledge necessary for improving academic achievement for their diverse learners. Teachers in this urban district, later identified as the second most segregated for Latino students in the country (Vaznis 2010), worked with high numbers of Puerto Rican students and increasing numbers of newcomer students from across the globe. The mission of the program sought to help teachers understand how to explicitly teach language and literacy, in a way that valued the linguistic and cultural resources of these students and their families. The website described the program as holding a, 'theoretical framework ... grounded in a critical, praxis oriented understanding of teaching, learning, assessment and school change', leading to, 'school-based practices that draw on linguistic and cultural resources, to accomplish academic, social and political work that matters to them and communities to which [students] belong'. With the focus on the students in the district, the crux of the mission was to prepare inservice teachers to develop an informed and 'critical' stance in order to accomplish the mission. We worked with a cohort of inservice teachers, primarily Latina and White women, teaching at district elementary and middle schools who were seeking degrees and additional licensure as ESL and/or reading specialists.

The practice of a critical pedagogy was the impetus for our involvement in the alliance of educators sponsoring this program. Freire challenges educators to develop a 'critical praxis' – that is to come into consciousness by recognizing that we are all subjects of our own lives. Basically, humans produce and transform reality together

(Kamberelis and Dimitriadis 2005). As course instructors following this belief, we intended to work collaboratively 'with' the program's teachers to support their development of the research skills and literacy expertise necessary to talk back productively to state and district mandates that devalued their work. Based on personal experiences as teachers ourselves, we worked from a perspective that 'no one asks teachers' about how to improve schools and, in addition, 'no one asks the students about what they know and can do' when implementing reforms. Thus, as we began this first course on *Practitioner Research* we not only asked teachers to respond to negative press but also asked them to interrupt the expectations that limited teachers' roles, positioning them as passive implementers of prescriptive curriculum (Altwerger et al. 2004). We urged them to gain expertise as literacy practitioners so that their knowledge of content, language, and the students themselves could be foregrounded to inform the district literacy curriculum.

Early on we were challenged to rethink our stance as 'critical educators' when many in this group resisted what we intended to be 'empowering' course practices, assigning readings written by teacher researchers. Vocal resistance emerged in responses to one assigned book chapter, written by a high school literacy educator. Arguing that the author used 'academic language' disconnected from real experiences in real schools, one teacher directly addressed the author's charge to keep abreast of the educational literature with the response, 'I'd rather not.' Realizing early on that teachers' realities afforded little support or time to challenge current practices, or seek out new knowledge independently, we felt called to adopt what Fendler (2003) calls a 'vigilant critique' on our practices as teacher educators. That is, as critical teacher educators we needed to engage with the dilemmas we faced:

- How could we avoid endorsing perspectives that reinforced institutional norms and devalued the knowledge of teachers and their students, while also honoring the realities and experiences that these teachers brought to the class community?
- How could we avoid imposing a 'critical' stance that was simply an imposition of our own ideology, rather than a collaborative creation of new knowledge intended to achieve program goals leading to 'academic, social, and political work' that 'mattered' to the teachers and, most importantly, to their students?

Freire's work focuses on language and the generative meanings attached to language used in society. Central to this work (and ours) are the identification of 'generative words' and reflection on how words function to make meaning within social and political contexts. The purpose of this analysis is to share how we as critical educators, committed to what we defined as 'critical praxis', found it necessary to interrogate our own understanding of these words as we attempted to implement our mission. Developing a critical praxis, according to Freire, is engaging in cycles of action and reflection with the goal of social transformation. Thus, we addressed our dilemmas through cycles of our own action research and used tools of critical discourse analysis as part of our pedagogy and reflection over a period of time spanning three semesters, beginning with the *Practitioner Research* course and extending through two subsequent inquiry-focused courses: *Content Literacy for L1 and L2* and *Reading for L1 and L2*. The latter two courses culminated in a conference where the same cohort of teachers presented classroom research publicly to district administrators, colleagues, university faculty, and university students. This analysis afforded the opportunity to question our dilemmas and to continually 're-search' our participation along with the cohort teachers whom we expected to be critical 'researchers' of their practices.

Class community as a 'contact zone'

The teachers' resistance created a necessary reexamination of our pedagogy and a need to question our own critical approach more deeply. In retrospect, we were pushed to recognize the class community as a 'contact zone'. Coined by Mary Louise Pratt (1991, 33), contact zones are 'social spaces where cultures meet, clash, and grapple with each other, often in contexts of highly asymmetrical relations of power'. The construct of a contact zone was useful to our learning, as it provides a frame not only to reconsider the model of community that both we and our students rely on in teaching and theorizing, but simultaneously to examine how language was taken up, mixed up, and remixed into new texts as our course progressed. In keeping with a critical pedagogy, we felt impelled to respond to the 'I'd rather not' message by initiating a discussion in a subsequent class, which as practitioner researchers ourselves we asked to videotape for further analysis. In this class session, we invited teachers to both take up the chapter's challenge as well as present their own perspectives on the role of research and teachers' work related to research. The discussion challenged our view about teacher-authored articles. Many felt that although we attempted to share a teachers' perspective, that perspective was not very different from the message in more 'academic' articles where the language used positioned teachers as receivers of research and did not acknowledge the actual 'realities' of classrooms in which they taught. We questioned how articles of this type did get published and realized that in order to meet standards of educational publication and peer review, adopting language of the academy was often a necessary reality. Yet, was there value for teachers in struggling with unfamiliar language, especially if that language challenged them to new learning for the benefit of their students? Some teachers did speak up and agree with this latter perspective while others did not, so that several perspectives became visible for consideration, including ours as instructors.

The notion of a 'contact zone' helps us to envision the class sessions as spaces created by interactions between all participants and consider how the language of interactions positioned participants, including us, and how the effects of power within these interactions resulted in learning. As we viewed the videotaped discussion, noting how various perspectives were voiced, it was immediately obvious that not all voices participated publicly. In a section of the room sat a group of four Latina teachers quietly communicating among themselves but not once speaking out in the discussion. Without the videotape, we would have missed this. Interestingly, Carmen was a member of this group.

Acting on the resistance and stepping back to understand the difference that existed within this interactional space also brought the complexity of this space into a clearer focus. Participation structures were varied and simultaneous. For example, small groups interacted while the larger group 'give and take' between instructor and students occurred. We realized the temptation to acknowledge only those who participated in our direct agenda – the instructor-directed conversation, while ignoring other forms of participation that were less visible. These included the small group on the video, personal one-on-one conversations before, during, and after class, and the written reflections, responses, and assignments. Carmen's participation provides an example of rich learning that occurred for her and for us that would have remained unacknowledged without a 'vigilant critique' of our own teaching in relationship to our students.

Carmen's participation: remixing language, retaining control

We realized that Carmen was fairly quiet in class but took time during breaks or after sessions to seek an instructor out to personally share ideas, stories of her life, her teaching goals, and stories about her students. We also reflected on other outlets for Carmen's participation provided by the course structure. Writings, such as the newspaper response above, along with various responses intended to support and extend the classroom research process were periodically assigned. Although we had responded with primary feedback each time Carmen submitted these assignments, the intention of that feedback was to support her process of learning classroom inquiry. However, 're-reading' these documents later, with a critical discourse lens, was equally informative for our own learning.

Specifically attending to language in her written assignments, we noticed that she was actively participating and 'writing herself into the conversation' (Dyson 1991, 7). The work of Bakhtin reminds us that all interactions involve bits of other 'utterances' that have existed in the past and are picked up, revoiced, and remixed as present texts are constructed. We examined the discourse patterns in three examples of Carmen's course writings that included: responses to readings including the teacher-authored article and the newspaper story, her initial 'storyline' from a first attempt to analyze classroom data, and a summary statement after completion of the classroom research project for this course. Interestingly, throughout her writing, Carmen developed her autonomy through what Dyson terms 'reflective play', by mixing discourses that we regarded as ideologically different in the same text to create a message for her reader as well as work new ideas against those which were familiar or more widely used.

In the excerpts below we illustrate how Carmen used language to position herself differently as she built intersecting points of view drawn from her experiences as a district teacher, English language learner (ELL) and student in the master's program. Throughout, she maintained control of her message using strongly voiced exclamations (e.g., 'it is exhausting!'), centering herself and at times her fellow teachers through a first person use of 'I' or 'we' pronouns as well as appropriating institutional language (e.g., terms such as *intervention* or *proficiency*) and mixing these discursively with words or phrases from the practitioner research readings (e.g., *the questions evolving*[2]) within her documents.

In some places she positioned herself, Carmen, as a compliant teacher with not enough expertise, an example seen earlier in the newspaper response. She told of trying harder to find prescribed programs or outside specialist services that would improve student learning. Despite the rich funds of knowledge she held about ELL students, her first research plan involved capitulating to the expertise of others (e.g., a pathologist):

> The principal called and informed me that she spoke to a chapter I teacher, Ms. P, who is a pathologist, and she agreed to work with us. Later on these children were tested to see what English stage they were. Ms. P felt that they were not that bad but they surely needed some help. After that she never came back and that was that. A few years passed and I think this is the time and opportunity to approach her once again.

In this statement and others that emerged across all the writing, Carmen continued to include dominant institutional terminology, such as identifying English language learners as those without 'basic language skills', or considering an 'intensive phonemic awareness program' as 'early intervention'. Even as she changed her initial plan, began to look closely through an experiential and critical lens at her students, and eventually used her own research findings from a later course to challenge district practices, she was careful to include the institutionally required data (e.g., test scores) and continued to measure the 'proficiency levels' of her students' academic performance. Even as her ideas about curriculum shifted through this course, she understood the importance of continuing to communicate her research findings using language that would be understood by a district and state audience.

Simultaneously, Carmen mirrored her colleagues' resistance to the course expectations in her writing. Although she did not contribute to public discussion, in her writing she created parallel critiques of how she and colleagues were positioned by district expectations as well as the university program expectations that she felt were disconnected from the realities of her job. After complaining about administrators who ignored the complexity of teachers' work and did not appreciate the time it took to teach, in several texts she argued that teachers are always researchers, without the need for the extra work required in the course. One example is found below:

> Research happens constantly and automatically. If something doesn't function or fail, we [teachers] look for other alternative ways in how to approach the students until they get it. But we don't have to take tedious notes, nevertheless, to keep records of it. At this time, I am experiencing overwhelming feelings of tension and stress with this class work. We don't have the time and it is a struggle to keep up with it.

As another example of this critique, she indirectly gives advice to us as instructors about the clarity of our assignments:

> Nowadays administrators are taking every bit of time we have to fulfill the students and school needs to pass the assessments. At this moment I don't know how to approach all the work we have to do for this class. Or maybe, it is that the class assignments were not distributed properly.

Throughout her writing, we also found examples of Carmen aligning herself with a larger group that represents 'good teachers'. In the excerpt below, she addressed the power of teachers who stick together, suggesting this solidarity as a force for addressing their deprofessionalization by others. In addition, she named another issue that devalued her professional identity. This was the tension between 'mainstream' classroom teachers and ESL specialists, one that often remained 'unspoken' and, as we will discuss later, was rooted in views about race and language within the school and community:

> To make a long story short, there are many other teaching approaches: classroom organization, consistency of routines, etc. that easily could help improve students' achievement, making them feel successful. Do you think this is hard to do? It is exhausting! I have experienced that, in many cases, mainstream teachers are not willing to do all this. It takes lots of time and energy, but it can be done. We need to stick together, and help one another, especially in grade level ... where we can keep what works and discard what does not.

Within the contested space of the practitioner research course, Carmen, an ESL specialist, not only wrote from different positions, she also engaged in what Dyson calls a process of 'borrowing and learning'. Similar to the genres used by academic writers, who engage in ongoing conversation where they draw on the work of others to create new learning, Carmen appropriated phrases and technical terminology and incorporated them to stretch her own purposes rather than comply with others. Despite her ongoing critique, she increasingly utilized new language from the practitioner research literature (e.g., *questions evolving* and *triangulation*) and incorporated it in her own time and in her own terms. One of our favorite examples is found in the second excerpt below in her summary of 'triangulation' as 'salvation!':

> I notice that when a question evolves, others follow it. If something doesn't function, I try another approach. But it is much easier when you do it automatically, without having to take the time, time that we don't have, to take notes, analyze, and document it.
>
> Triangulation is the use of multiple sources to support findings. This was my salvation! I followed it and was able to lay out my sources and starting finding how one thing was agreeing with another. After analyzing all the data I came to the conclusion that despite K's lack of English language proficiency, she has found various methods to learn.

What was compelling across her written work was her confident and direct voice, especially present when she wrote from her positions of competence in solidarity with fellow teachers and also as a person with experiences in learning a new language while navigating schooling. In her writing she also showed strength by taking up positions that tended to be publicly devalued in society and the schools. These included those of knowledgeable teacher and a knowledgeable ESL teacher who was bilingual, demonstrated below:

> Observing this child makes me think about my own learning skills as an English language learner. Maybe that is why I sympathize with and enjoy so much teaching ELL students. So much time is spent observing and discussing negative aspects of teaching; we tend to overlook what is positive and extraordinary about our students. It is encouraging to stop and appreciate a student like K.

Through sampling, creating, and remixing texts, Carmen retained control of how she was positioned as an educator while also stretching herself and us to new ways of thinking. She achieved critical purposes that included reflection on her own 'funds of knowledge' (Moll et al. 1992) in relationship to her current position. She also positioned herself as a knowledgeable participant as she gave feedback to us as course instructors demonstrating how she was making meaning of the course activities and goals, including insights based on both her struggles and her perceived benefits. Finally, she offered an important perspective on the position of students who are newcomers attempting to navigate public schools while also learning English; this perspective was made possible due to her personal experience as a Puerto Rican woman ESL teacher within a school setting. In doing so, she 'named the world' and helped those of us in the contact zone of the course who did not have access to those vital experiences to better understand students' realities.

This initial cycle of investigation into resistance provided concrete examples that encouraged us to be vigilant and not to inadvertently erase difference while attempting to build a critically focused learning community. Carmen's initial texts provide prime examples of her authority in controlling her learning through her use of language and also how the language of the inquiry course offered her tools for deeper perspectives on what she already knew. In subsequent cycles, we continued this 're-search' through questioning the role of reflective practice.

What is the use of a reflection tool?

Our first analysis cycle reinforced the need for 'vigilant critique' to prevent the unconscious positioning of teachers as subservient despite our intentions for course participation to be 'empowering'. Fendler (2003, 23) reminds us that, 'the subservience of the teacher is based primarily on the observation that expert researchers rarely listen to teachers when they develop policy and teaching guidelines'. Our program goals were designed to promote teachers' agency through challenging the effects of 'reform' efforts that rarely listened to teachers or assessed the social, cultural, or linguistic 'funds of knowledge' unique to students. Our intention was to support teachers' learning of language theory that would encourage them to combine explicit language instruction with complex learning in content areas. Especially important to our critical pedagogy was that this instruction would not reproduce a delivery model of new ideas and practices but instead include attention to culturally and linguistically relevant pedagogy. Yet, at the same time as our courses were held, teachers were being asked to implement a district-wide 'lesson planning' system, a response to state-level criticism that was intended to regulate the pacing and timing of curriculum across all classrooms in the large district, with little attention to the diversity of the students within. Therefore, our course goals conflicted with strong workplace messages that pressured teachers to standardize their instruction as well as the teachers' ongoing struggle with time and overload expressed in the earlier course.

Keeping this in mind, for our second course, we invited teachers to design a reflection tool that synthesized course learning with their classroom inquiry in a way that best fitted the time and spaces of their teaching lives. This 'reflective teaching journal' was included in the criteria for constructing an inquiry portfolio as they taught and researched a content unit. The stated purpose of the journal was written by a third course instructor, Andres,[3] who collaborated with us during this time and is excerpted below:

> I have experienced that if you make the journal your own, if you use it as a resource and not just as a requirement, it becomes invaluable for your reflection. The idea is that [later when you are analyzing data] you will come back to the journal with fresh eyes, searching for illuminating moments ... the journal format is by no means mandatory. If you have experienced that other options work for you to accomplish similar purposes, feel free to use what you feel more comfortable with.

The journals revealed similar 'reflective play' on the part of many teachers that provided insights and opportunities for us as instructors to see our own ideas in relationship to those of our students as we provided feedback that often extended further into ongoing dialogues.

'Reflective play'

In creating these reflective texts, many teachers took the opportunity to engage in the same reflective play with ideas and language found in Carmen's initial writings. For example, Julia, a White bilingual classroom teacher, reflected in both English and Spanish at one point, wondering:

> *No comprendo porque muchas de mis estudiantes teinan problemas con escribiendo en Español.*
> [I don't understand why so many of my students have problems with writing in Spanish.]

For Julia and others, reflections spanned several categories that were not necessarily distinct and not hierarchical but provided a heuristic for our review. We called these: (1) technical aspects of teaching (e.g., included lesson plans and teaching ideas or 'to do' lists – sometimes directly cut and pasted from other sources into the journal); (2) process notes (e.g., diagrams to work out teaching ideas or data collection linked to their research); (3) self-reflection (e.g., listing assumptions or self-discovery – 'I could have done better at'); and (4) social or critical questions (e.g., insights directly from observations of their students' learning, often in relation to diversity and/or political contexts).

An example of the latter is also found in Julia's journal:

> Very interesting – all my students from P.R. [Puerto Rico] put the flag on almost all assignments. They truly identify themselves more as P.R. vs. Americans and do not seem to care if visuals are supposed to be included in assignments. They simply put them in all the time ... It's becoming more and more clear to me that my students need to connect to work on a personal level in order to produce. Very important: I tried using a worksheet on conflict resolution, introducing key vocabulary and using real life situations. They love role playing and using their native language to discuss and plan in English.

Teaching in a state with 'English Only' legislation, where the dominant social message is to erase primary languages in favor of English, Julia used the reflective process to develop a lesson that affirmed her Puerto Rican students' identity and primary language while scaffolding their learning of the English necessary for academic success in US schools. The use of the journal for this purpose also highlighted the expertise of teachers who themselves had control of multiple languages and demonstrated the power afforded by their linguistic and cultural experiences in a social and political environment where these were publicly devalued.

Marie Claire, a White English dominant classroom teacher, also used her journal to play with the linguistic ideas from the course curriculum by linking them to observations of her students and her own 'funds of knowledge' in reading and literacy. Similar to Carmen's writing above, she mixed observational language with technical terminology, developing a diagram for observing her students:

> Ah ha! ESOL students are vocal about language challenges; [a] supportive and fun environment encourages children to ask ?'s, experiment with language, mimic and copy, make connections. ESOL students need direct grammar instructions to more successfully control the language and gain skills and confidence. My training was more whole language focused where the focus was on content [but there was an incorrect assumption] that grammar and phonics would be absorbed.

After filling in her diagram with student observations, she added:

> [Maybe I should] do a lesson that compares and contrasts ABC book language and pictures (multi-modal analysis)?

Marie Claire's comments demonstrate reflexivity in understanding how her deep experience as a literacy teacher should be extended to make sure that her ELLs were not expected to simply 'absorb' the grammar they experienced in their literacy curriculum; instead they required a combination of meaningful curriculum and explicit language teaching. A course structure that encouraged teachers to be the designers of their learning in ways that 'mattered' to them and their students, for the most part, demonstrated the opportunities available for curricular reform that encouraged teachers to 'mix' their current experiential and professional knowledge with new learning about content, pedagogy, and close observation of their students' learning needs. This was a stark contrast to patterns of professional development where ongoing cycles of instructional prescriptions continue to ignore what teachers and students already know and can do.

Sharing 'what matters' in public, interrogating what counts as 'critical'?

Freire talks of 'limit situations' as those situations that people cannot imagine themselves beyond. The language embedded within cultures naturalizes people's sense of oppression. Applying this thinking to the positioning of teachers in urban schools is relevant. Although teachers spend hours interacting with students in classrooms, dominant practices in school culture rarely support their development as leading agents of change (Kamberelis and Dimitriadis 2005). That teachers, rather than outside experts or administrators, would facilitate a district-wide conference was a culture shift that was not easy for us or for the teachers in our program.

At the same time, as the organizers of the culminating conference and as instructors of several courses focused on preparing teachers to facilitate at this conference, we needed to remain aware of the power relations inherent in this situation. Elizabeth Ellsworth's (1989, 301) question, 'What diversity do we silence in the name of "liberatory pedagogy?"', is relevant to us as a guide throughout cycles of teaching and reflecting. Having evidence available to check ourselves, such as chains of emails between instructors and teachers, feedback we gave on the portfolios (including the reflection journals) before teachers began to revise for their presentations, teaching memos and classroom video – all provided important information about how we encouraged and discouraged ideas from teachers as they planned and presented. More specifically, we had to interrogate our own conceptualization of 'critical' as we interacted with teachers who prepared for what was definitely a new role.

We will return to the two teachers quoted early in the article, Carmen and Dyan, to illustrate our need to look beyond the dichotomy of 'instructor' and 'students' (as a group) and, instead, look at how our actions and power dynamics intersected with those of each teacher, among the cohort group, and within the expanded contact zone of the conference that included the presence of principals and administrators as well as our university colleagues. A generative phrase that helps us investigate the challenges faced by each teacher is 'high expectations for all learners', found below in an excerpt from the conference program:

> Today ... teachers, district administrators, and university literacy researchers come together to engage in conversations focused on the learning of [The City's] Public School students. In each session, teachers will provide a glimpse into what student learning actually looks like in their elementary and middle school classrooms. They will offer brief presentations about specific students' learning based upon the data collected while teaching content units. Afterwards, session participants will be invited to share ideas for expanding this focus forward in classrooms, in school buildings, in the district, in the state, and at the university. Connecting content and language learning is KEY in creating an environment of *'high expectations for all learners'*. (1)

The phrase 'high expectations for all learners' held different meanings within the district. This phrase, clearly highlighted on the district website, could be linked to the forces of standardization and alternatively could be interpreted in accordance with our program's mission of developing: 'school-based practices that draw on linguistic and cultural resources, to accomplish academic, social and political work that matters to them and communities to which [students] belong'. Both teachers found it necessary to navigate these conceptualizations as they made meaning of their research for their students, themselves, and more publicly for a combined district and university audience.

Dyan: reminding us to 'remain vigilant' of teachers' vulnerability

Dyan's reflections and interactions with us as instructors continually pointed to a competing influence, embodied by a strong new principal who valued compliance with standardization efforts in the district. An ongoing tension for Dyan throughout the research and presentation process was her emerging experience with critical pedagogy, juxtaposed with strong pressure from her principal not to diverge from a 'one-size fits all' paced curriculum guide. For example, during her research process Dyan quoted one of her special education students' responses to a math assignment, '[I] could not go to the mall and by [sic] things because people might not give [me] the right change.' Dyan's reaction prompted her to diverge from the teacher's manual script in the 'money' unit she was teaching to respond. She reflected:

> I am to teach grade level materials but to find a way to teach it so the students understand when they are actually two years below grade level. Just once I want my students to be able to go somewhere and do one thing that they are confident doing. Knowing that when they walk into a store with $10.00 and spend money and know exactly the amount they should get back, and if they do not get the right amount back, to be able to communicate that to whoever is there without reservation or questions.

Development of a unit that involved both learning to communicate about money, while also learning the mathematics of money, would look very different from the commercial math program that had a less contextual focus. Dyan understood that her principal's mandate 'everyone on the same page' was filled with good intentions (i.e., not to water down the curriculum for students with special needs), yet she found the principal inflexible in understanding how a context-based unit could actually provide both rigor and relevance for her students. During the research and revision period, Dyan engaged with Andres and Elizabeth through email about this tension. Taking up an instructor's suggestion, she initiated several conversations about 'money and power' in her classroom, and the richness of the conversation among her special education students surprised her. When the time came to present her findings in public to an audience that included her principal, Dyan presented an 'implementation' of some math-writing lessons that she found helpful in connecting to the math curriculum; however, she chose not to present the critical conversations with her class or use those conversations to further revise her teaching. She noted in a discussion following the conference:

> I don't think she [the principal] would have liked the money and power thing...I know Pat and Andres would have loved it, but my principal wouldn't. So I [focused] mostly on what we had designated in our school improvement plan. I gave in to the pressure!

Clearly, we initially considered Dyan's decision as backing away from a critical stance; yet, she did push herself to respond to her students and adapted instruction when she witnessed her 'two years below grade level' special education students performing in ways that the prescriptive curricula did not invite – that is, communicating in complex ways about power and money. Although she tempered her public presentation, it stretched the prescribed curriculum by combining math instruction with language education, something she understood was greatly needed by those students. It was necessary for us to reflect on the reasons why some teachers felt the need to navigate away from challenging the district system. Clifford (1988, cited in Kamberelis and Dimitriadis 2005) suggests learning to operate according to a 'hermeneutics of vulnerability'. While this term was created to describe the challenges of the critical researcher, we feel it also applies to us as critical teacher educators. That is, we are called to keep the multiple and contradictory positioning of all participants visible, in this case, respecting the vulnerability that many teachers faced when adopting the ideology of student-centered, critical pedagogy. As another teacher, Milli, stated about such tensions:

> Now it feels like our whole audience is different ... so we've learned through scaffolding with our peers but this feels like putting yourself on the line. I'm saying you have to have a respect for administration. You have to have a respect for your job. There's so many things on the balance that you sort of want to make it look, basically, you want to make it look GOOD, even though there are 'oh no' moments. You may be reluctant to show them.

Carmen: creating solidarity to challenge the system

The tensions surrounding forces for standardization were visible both in the class and later in the dialogue conversations. However, many other administrators and principals were quite interested in learning more about literacy practices to meet the needs of the ELLs in their schools. Each teacher negotiated her presentation differently. Carmen was one who made the decision to 'publicly' challenge district policy. Carmen chose to challenge the system with clear and well-presented evidence that indicated that the current 'hands-on' inquiry science curriculum was not meeting the needs of ELLs in her program. Her presentation emerged as she took ownership of the coursework by creating a research portfolio, but, interestingly, she completely ignored the 'reflective journal' assignment. Instead, she sought feedback, frequently initiated through direct contact with peers and instructors during small-group workshop sessions as well as through email. For example, after creating a chart with her students about the 'life cycle of insects', she touched base to get feedback and reflect on next steps to help her ELLs to connect the visual with language needed for a written explanation. Her quest for excellence was demonstrated in the continual give and take between course instructors and Carmen as she slowly crafted her research, focusing what she already knew about the academic needs of L2 English learners and new ideas she was gaining from the course content. She was flexible, communicating in Spanish with Andres as well as in English with us (Pat and Elizabeth). Below is an excerpt from an email where she followed up with Andres, asking for the feedback sheet she 'lost' and also attaching a draft of her *PowerPoint* research presentation. Andres took time not only to provide the feedback sheet but to edit and give suggestions for revising her work:

> *Hola Andres! Como te encuentras? Andres, tu recuerdas el paper en que tu nos entregastes con los comentarios sobre nuestro portfolio? Pues sabes que? Lo perdi en la*

clase. Podrias enviarme una copia via-email? Aqui te envio lo que e hecho con el power point para la presentacion.

[Hi Andres! How do you feel? Andres, you remember the paper you provided us with feedback on our portfolio? Well guess what? I lost it in class. Could you send me a copy via-email? Here I'm also sending you what I've done on my *PowerPoint* presentation.]

Dear Carmen, Take a look at my suggestions. You need a video to show and illustrate, perhaps scaffold the language of explanation. You also need to highlight the [performance assessment] more in your presentation. You also need a slide in which you make your main point by linking it to the data you showed. I'm also sending you the feedback I gave you on the portfolio. (Andres)

Due to Carmen's initiative, she and another teacher had drafts of their *PowerPoints* created well ahead of the class. We asked both of these teachers if they would share their work with the larger group as 'models' for the revision process. In her first public sharing of her work, in front of the class and instructors, Carmen provided clear evidence that the stance of the content-only science embraced by the district needed to be infused with explicit language teaching. Her classroom data, illustrating improved writing by her students, supported her point. An excerpt from her slide show arguing this point can be found in Figure 1.

Carmen's presentation received a mixed reaction from the class that illuminated a second set of power differentials that as instructors we had glimpsed from time to time. Pat's memo after the workshop class explains:

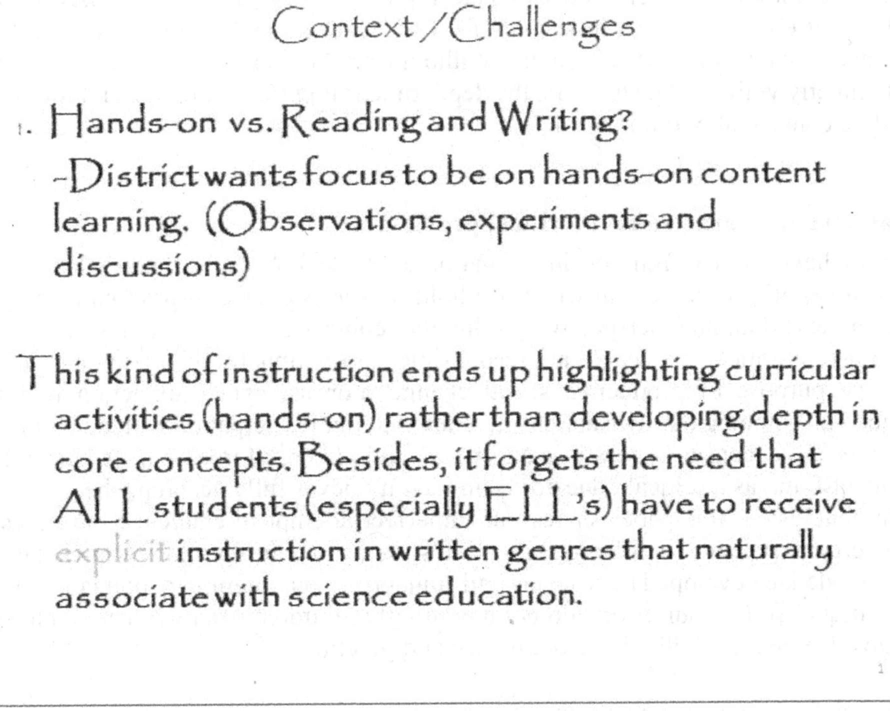

Context/Challenges

1. Hands-on vs. Reading and Writing?
   – District wants focus to be on hands-on content learning. (Observations, experiments and discussions)

This kind of instruction ends up highlighting curricular activities (hands-on) rather than developing depth in core concepts. Besides, it forgets the need that ALL students (especially ELL's) have to receive explicit instruction in written genres that naturally associate with science education.

Figure 1. Carmen's slide.

> The class itself was one of four 'workshop' classes [focused on] revising PowerPoint presentations to 'show' their research. Two teachers from the class, one white teacher and one Latina teacher, had been particularly involved emailing, seeking feedback from the instructors and project assistants, and developing innovations during the revision cycle. The instructors asked them if they would talk to the group using their revision process as a scaffold for other teachers. When the time came, the white teacher's presentation to the group was attended to completely by other teachers in the class ... during the Latina teacher's presentation however side conversations developed and fewer paid attention. In the eyes of the instructor, both presenters had strong voices, good ideas ... Afterwards, a white teacher came to me asking me to 'speak to' the Latina teacher about her strong language critiquing the science program. Privately, I questioned whether this was an issue of race and language discrimination, questioning what 'right' an ESL teacher had to critique the more powerful science department.

Carmen's case illuminates an intersecting set of pressures connected to race, language, culture, and power that also served to reduce autonomy for teachers and students within the system and within our course culture. The workshop events raised further questions about what Carmen had 'named' in her earlier writing, a present but unacknowledged separation between classroom teachers and ESL specialists. It also raised questions of status connected to different 'disciplinary' departments within the system. In asking her not to challenge the science department, did her colleague unconsciously 'name' unwritten value systems connected to students who were ELLs? What further work can be done to address these barriers productively?

We chose not to 'speak' to Carmen, whose presentation at the conference was informative for all. Interestingly, we have used Carmen's presentation subsequently in teaching and at conferences as it makes a clear and understandable point about the need for combining content and language for ELLs. Also, the issues raised by her work about equity of status in schools for ESL teachers and ELLs inform our own subsequent work as teacher educators. Without Carmen's initiative to 'reflect' on her work directly with us as instructors, the depth of learning for her, for us, and for others could be considerably diminished.

What have we learned about 'critical praxis'?

What we have learned from this interrogation of 'critical praxis' is that teacher education is a negotiated process in which we hold power as course instructors to support or ignore less-dominant perspectives within the 'contact zones' of our classes. Choosing to take a critical stance, we are responsible for continually theorizing and acting with the purpose of productive social change. For us, cycles of action research included questioning our own actions in relation to our participation with our students. This raised our consciousness in many ways, and also reinforced our understanding that identifying as a critical educator is an identity never fully accomplished.

In conclusion, this paper shares our imperfect attempt to challenge ourselves to create critical practice in order to shift value systems in education to acknowledge the rich knowledge developed by teachers and students. In our attempt to maintain a 'vigilant critique' so that our efforts do not unwittingly reinforce what we seek to change, we have learned the following from theory and practice:

- Take care not to unconsciously erase difference, even when it is tempting to attend only to those who participate in our agenda.

- Accessing difference is difficult but enhanced through attention to language. Freire's notion of 'generative words' helped us to identify language (such as 'high expectations') that holds power within the social spaces that we occupy with our students but whose multiple meanings remain unquestioned.
- Using tools of discourse analysis helps to track 'reflective play' with language and ideas. Bakhtin's notion of 'speaking and writing oneself into the conversation' directed our attention to the mixing of language within our course and subsequently a flexible shift in positions and identities opening new opportunities for learning.
- Pathways to meaning making that were most effective for students' purposes were not always immediately obvious. For example, Carmen's decision to forgo public comments or, later on, her reflective teaching journal took other forms that not only accomplished set goals but often generated deeper insights.

Peter Murrell calls to university teacher educators, especially those who prepare teachers to work in urban schools, to assume a 'stance of humility'. He reminds us that the 'measure of our success as agents for change is not the expertise we bring as university people, but rather our capacity to learn in the company of others' (Murrell 2001, 33). What we have learned through this questioning of our critical perspective has led to richer learning in the company of the teachers we serve.

Notes
1. All teachers we worked with signed Human Subjects permission through the Federal Title VII Career Ladder Grant and a Title III 'No Child Left Behind' Grant that funded our work.
2. Appropriated from course reading of Chapter 2 in Hubbard and Power (1999).
3. We acknowledge the work of Dr Andres Ramirez who collaborated in, developed, and co-taught the two courses in the second sequence.

References

Altwerger, B., P. Arya, L. Jin, N.L. Jordan, B. Laster, P. Martens, G.P. Wilson, and N. Wiltz. 2004. When research and mandates collide: The challenges and dilemmas of teacher education in the era of NCLB. *English Education* 36, no. 2: 119–33.

Dyson, A. 1991. A Bakhtinian buzz about teacher talk: Discourse matters in 'What difference does difference make?' *English Education* 35, no. 1: 6–20.

Ellsworth, E. 1989. Why doesn't this feel empowering? Working through the repressive myths of critical pedagogy. *Harvard Education Review* 59, no. 3: 297–325. (Republished in *The education feminism reader*, ed. L. Stone, 300–27. 1994. New York: Routledge.)

Fendler, L. 2003. Teacher reflection in a hall of mirrors: Historical influences and political reverberations. *Educational Researcher* 32, no. 3: 16–25.

Hubbard, R., and B. Power. 1999. *Living the questions.* Portland, ME: Stenhouse.

Kamberelis, G., and G. Dimitriadis. 2005. Focus groups: Strategic articulations of pedagogy, politics, and inquiry. In *Handbook of qualitative research*, ed. N.K. Denzin and Y.S. Lincoln, 887–907. Thousand Oaks, CA: Sage.

Moll, L.C., C. Amanti, D. Neff, and N. Gonzalez. 1992. Funds of knowledge for teaching: Using a qualitative approach to connect homes and classrooms. *Theory into Practice* 31, no. 2: 132–41.

Murrell, P. 2001. *The community teacher.* New York: Teachers College Press.

Pratt, M.L. 1991. Arts of the contact zone. In *Profession 91*, ed. P. Franklin, 33–40. New York: MLA.

Vaznis, J. 2010. Area school segregation called rife. *Boston Globe*, September 20. http://pqasb.pqarchiver.com/boston/access/2141628761.html?FMT=ABS&date=Sep+20%2C+2010.

Recovering from 'yo mama is so stupid': (en)gendering a critical paradigm on Black feminist theory and pedagogy

Rochelle Brock

School of Education, Indiana University Northwest, 3400 Broadway, 303 Hawthorn Hall, Gary, IN 46408, USA

This article offers an analysis of the dozens using Black feminist theory. The dozens are a ritualized verbal game of insults that historically have used sexual offenses against Black women as the vehicle for insults. Rather than simply viewing the dozens as a cultural phenomenon, the article draws a connection between its occurrence in West Africa, the West Indies, slave communities, and post enslavement and attempts to understand the various changes and the connection of the dozens to Black female devaluation. Through dialog with Oshun, the author deconstructs the historical and cultural significance of the dozens, placing it in a constructed conversation methodology. Importantly, the article shows how deconstruction of the dozens can be used as a pedagogical tool leading students to a deeper and more thorough understanding of a taken-for-granted cultural phenomenon.

Introduction

Writing is an extension of my soul. I string letters together to make words and words to craft sentences, and sentences to create an intricate dance into theory and my truth. In my dance, self and text become one. The movement of the words pushes life into the text, which is where the text finds the freedom to 'reinscribe experience' and bring 'newly discovered meanings to the [my] reader' (Denzin 1998, 322). When we structure our writing in ways that lay itself bare, we create a world of unforeseen possibilities where previous meanings morph into something new and unique (Brock 2005; Denzin and Lincoln 1998; Richardson 1998). I continuously aim for three-dimensional writing where words do not sit motionless and flat on the page but instead are filled with all of the emotions I experience when writing; the words take on a life of their own; they lead where I need to go. In this way, I unearth the meaning and purpose of what I am writing through the actual act of writing. Writing is personal. I find joy and sadness in writing. I become one with the words, and those words mirror whatever angst or intellectual breakthroughs I experience.

The personal method of writing has been discussed by many qualitative researchers (Brock 1999, 2005; Denzin and Lincoln 1998; Fine 1998; Kincheloe 2005; Richardson

1998). I take what I need from them; play with their theories, extracting those pieces that fit my purpose, always attempting to develop what is unique to me. I learn and teach best through dialog with others and importantly dialog with self. I have to creatively articulate the internal struggle that is central to my thought process. I have to write my truth, and my truth is the demystification that happens through dialog. My purpose is to experiment with the traditional format of academic writing as I deconstruct a cultural phenomenon within the African American community by considering it as a pedagogical activity for higher education. The current emphasis on standards and testing (Cavanagh 2005; Sternberg 2006) makes it too easy to set aside the socio-emotional and cognitive dimensions of education where 'real' learning and transformation occur. I take pieces of the real and the imagined and marry them into a story concerned with redirecting the boundaries about how I discuss and analyze *the dozens*. In my writing I create an 'other world', one in which the fluidity of past and present coalesces in the creation of a new present. Denzin and Lincoln (1998, 322) state that:

> [i]n writing, the writer creates the world. He or she fills it with real and fictional people. Their problems and their crisis are brought to life. Their lives gone out of control are vividly described. Their lives, suddenly illuminated with new meanings and new transformation of self, are depicted.

My purpose in this article is to analyze the dozens as a pedagogical site using Black feminist theory. Black feminist theory reconceptualizes all dimensions of the dialectic of oppression and activism of and by Black women, which forces me to see the misogyny inherent in the game. Black feminist theory gives voice to my analysis of the dozens because it allows me to use a specific way of knowing and experiencing the world from a Black woman's perspective as I study a Black cultural phenomenon. The epistemology of Black feminist theory utilizes those criteria important to me as a Black woman – dialog, experiential understanding, criticality and putting Black woman at the center of the discussion. It is especially useful in the study of the dozens because it has the ability to reinterpret what has already been done through new theoretical frameworks by beginning with the assumption that Black women's knowledge has been subjugated/suppressed and that Black women have the right and responsibility to reclaim, discover and reinterpret that which affects their reality. Moving toward this reinterpretation requires an epistemology centered in Black feminist theory. A Black feminist epistemology aims to raise the political consciousness of people with an Afrocentric worldview, placing them at the center of their own reality. In addition, a Black feminist epistemology challenges patriarchal structures and gender inequalities. I do not need to theorize about Black women using an epistemology that attempts to deny our humanity or existence. Instead, I choose to work within epistemological assumptions grounded in my history as a Black woman. I choose to learn from the all-too-often ignored and silenced theories of Black women regarding how we know and experience our world. Working within a Black feminist epistemological framework provides the space to challenge ontological questions of existence and being. How do I understand my realities as an objectified other? Where do I fight the battle for my selfhood? Where is my fight/struggle as a teacher, a scholar, a guide in the journey I take with my students? What can I learn from the historical exploitation of my sisters, and how does this knowledge influence/shape my pedagogy? These are all ontological questions asked as I search for a new way to understand the dozens from a pedagogical place.

The dozens

Known by many names[1] – rapping, signifying, giving rag, making mock, giving fatigue, capping, snaps and mother-rhyming – the dozens most often consist of references 'to alleged or incestuous activities of the opponent's mother, grandmother, daughters, sisters, wife, or other female relatives' (Foster 1986, 215). 'Yo mama is so stupid' represents a cornerstone of the joking game known as 'the dozens'. The dozens are a ritualized verbal game of insults that involve 'taunts and curses [which] are used to circumvent the point' (1986, 215). Take a listen:

> I hate to talk about your mother, she's a good old soul; she's got a leather-lined pussy and a brass asshole. Man tell your mama to stop coming around my house all the time. I'm tired of fucking her, and I think you should know that it ain't no accident you look like me. I fucked your mama for a solid hour. Baby came out screaming. Black Power.

Initially the topic of the dozens began for me when 'yo mama is so stupid' jokes were sent out on the Black Graduate Student listserv. Representing a cornerstone of 'the dozens', the jokes angered my womanist sensibilities, thereby forcing me to jot a quick reply. I made it short and simple, yet academic; ending with 'let's remember that the "dozens" began on the slave block as families were torn apart and think before we take part in our own subjugation'. Damn I was angry and determined to speak out against the misogyny and the continued devaluations of Black women that were part of the jokes. I also understood the power of words in the jokes that were supposedly benign. Anger becomes positive when you work within it so that it leads to an understanding of what initially caused the anger. When you allow anger to make you impotent, stop you from moving forward, then it is negative. But when the anger becomes a force that propels you into motion then go with it!

To this end, I received several pieces of electronic mail that exemplified this point. In particular, two of the responses were from Black male graduate students expressing their opinions on the jokes as well as my reaction to them. The first response, although seemingly naive, posited, 'Life is only as serious as you let it *not* be!' He seemed to postulate that life (here referring to the jokes) would only hurt me if I gave it the power to do so. Thus life's existential nature effectively reduced the underlying power and history the jokes possessed to construct and perpetuate Black female devaluation, to the level of non-effect. This comment was followed by a more detailed one stating, 'Some of it (the yo mama jokes) was definitely a mild form of self-hate. However, other parts were just fun between kids being kids.' After reading that message, I immediately called a sister-friend and together we questioned: What is *mild* self-hate? How can a person hate a small part of themselves and not hate the entire self? If the mild self-hate is just kids being kids, where does the hate go when those kids become adults?

These questions were the geneses of my need to critically deconstruct this game. My feelings about the jokes were visceral, but as an intellectual how could I epistemologically understand my reaction? I needed to tear apart the jokes and understand where my anger came from, and why for others the jokes were harmless. Was I being too sensitive? Where was the disconnect between what I heard and what others heard? I knew that deconstructing the dozens from a critical perspective would allow me to: (1) analyze the root philosophies germane to its emergence and sustainability; (2) understand the relation of the dozens to the societal structures in the African American community; (3) scrutinize the forms of patriarchy and misogyny within the dozens; and (4) examine the impact of this patriarchy on the concepts of Black womanhood.

Important to answering these questions as a teacher and a teacher educator, I needed to place my search within a pedagogical framework utilizing a critical theory.

Although I love and crave intellectual debate, the listserv argument was one-sided – patriarchal – and the scholar in me insisted on reframing how we looked at and talked about the dozens. I felt in my bones that it was misogynistic, and I knew there was a relationship between the devaluation of Black womanhood and the dozens. Perhaps not causal but definitely parallel, I saw the online discussion as one of those 'teachable moments' that we educators are constantly looking for. The dichotomy between my view and the view of others regarding the dozens was based on our opposing ideological lens. My job became to figure out how to analyze the dozens from a critical place so that I could support my visceral reaction. The most understandable way I found to do this was to look at how I would teach a critical analysis of the dozens to my students.

Often times, the ideological forces that anchor our decision-making processes remain hidden from consciousness. My goal is to ensure that these forces are made visible and that students understand the political and economic structures of domination and oppression and develop tools for change. Through a *Pedagogy of Wholeness* (Brock 1999), a greater understanding of those qualities important in a transformative education and teaching is possible. When pedagogy is transformative, students stop thinking of themselves in individualistic terms and instead as part of a community, realizing their freedom cannot come at the expense of the freedom of all people. They understand the historical connection between struggle and survival and then work to create a self-defined standpoint. A sociopolitical transformation allows a life transformation for the student to happen.

Ultimately students, especially those who are disenfranchised, understand the social, political and economic obstacles they are facing and have the tools to succeed in spite of those obstacles. When students are provided with the tools to analyze their everyday life through the lens of race, class and gender oppression they are able to think critically and to deconstruct the world. Sociopolitical transformation allows students to think politically and see the connections between thought and action because they have the criticality to understand historical occurrences. This understanding enables them to demystify the injustices of the world. Importantly, students possess the knowledge to interrogate those societal structures working against them, how they can combat the structures, and the form that fight will take.

A 'pedagogy of wholeness' affords a teacher the space to create a unique way of teaching and learning because it is not concerned with the traditional modalities of instruction. Instead a teacher utilizes whatever means they can because when we afford students the opportunity to use their constructive imagination (Bartlett 1928) they are able to grapple with intricate issues. According to Bartlett (1928, 85), in constructive imagination:

> [t]he material dealt with is not simply accepted or interpreted, but is taken as a problem and a challenge; and thus it is used and changed. Dominance is the essential temperamental characteristic of the genuine constructive imagination. It gathers its own material wherever it can, often searching wide fields; and what it gathers it shapes.

When I combine the three-dimensional writing discussed earlier with my understanding of constructed imagination, I accept the freedom to create whatever reality is needed. My reality is a constructed conversation (Brock 1999) between Oshun, the African goddess of love, and me. A constructed conversation methodology opens the space for dialog, a central epistemological tenet of Black feminist theory. According to Hill-Collins (1991, 212), 'A primary epistemological assumption underlying the use of dialogue in assessing knowledge claims is that connectedness rather than separation is an essential component of the knowledge validation process.' The connectedness dialog brings forth is reified (for me) when I use Oshun as my conduit to truth. She is my African past and my African American present. The dichotomy I love about Oshun is that she is both omniscient and questioning; at times she leads me to where I need to go in my thinking, and at other times I am the teacher providing her with my insights. Writing is typically experienced as a solitary act. Instead I call forth Oshun and together what was once solitary becomes a conversation between compañeras.

What follows is a glimpse into my created reality. In writing and conceptualizing this reality, I combine the factual with fiction. The theories and history are factual. The argument on the listserv that first brought up the topic of the dozens was real. The dream occurred just as I described it, and the frustration I was feeling prior to the dream was real. I wrap these facts in my conversation with Oshun, the entity that can feel and know those things that are difficult for me to touch. Please join my conversations with my innermost self as I bring to life the words that will engage the reader to participate in my struggle to articulate a feminist pedagogy as I deconstruct the dozens in a new way.

Making the subconscious conscious: my dream

When our mind is at rest we can at times see what has remained hidden from the conscious. For me a dream about my mother opened up a new way of thinking.

Rochelle: Oshun, do you dream?
Oshun: I am what you are; I do what you need me to do. Dreams are like a vessel into that which we cannot always name.
Rochelle: Not so long ago I had a dream. Prior to falling asleep all I could feel was the angst of being a Black woman living in a world hell-bent on silencing me at every turn. It was all making me so very, very tired and exhausted both emotionally and physically. Well, one night I laid in bed debating whether I should simply pull the covers over my head, block out the world, hide from reality, and try to find my private dreamland or be brave, roll out of bed, and face life (and by extension my computer) armed and ready for battle. Since both my mind and body were tired, doing battle seemed less interesting, as well as less do-able, than finding that magic happy place where all is right with the world.
Oshun: At times there are events in our lives that provide the impetus for us to search for such a place.
Rochelle: Yes. We may find that place either in music, food, drugs, or countless other vices. Since I am too cheap to buy much music, too vain to overeat, and too fearful of addiction to do drugs, I did the next best thing – I slept. More succinctly, I slept while temporarily hiding from the world of academia and all that identity forced me to deal with.

Stressed, upset, confused, alone, scared, tossing and turning, crying and screaming against the night, I fell asleep in the fetal position on my tiny sofa and dreamt about my mother. I reached back in my mind for a time and place different from where I now was; my childhood bedroom became where I re-remembered a different time. Although in my dream I was the age I am now, everyone else was younger. I saw myself brushing my little sister's hair when the phone rang. Answering it I heard my mother's voice but that was impossible – she was dead. I screamed into the receiver, 'You're dead, you're dead!' Calmly she replied, 'No, I am not. They lied to you.' I next saw myself in a hallway, running and there she was before me, looking younger and happier than when I had last seen her in the hospital as she waited to die. Always one to be stylish, mom was wearing a peach linen pantsuit embroidered around the collar with her hair pulled back in a bun. *Funny that I dream about my mother and remember vividly what she was wearing.* Again I screamed at her that she was dead; she could not be standing in front of me. Again she calmly told me that she was not dead, that I had been lied to, and she was here standing before me. I don't remember anything about my dream after that, although I feel it lasted much longer. I do remember that when I woke, peace was my blanket, wrapping me in a cocoon of tranquility. The angst that I experienced prior to falling asleep, if not completely gone, was at least manageable.

Oshun: Your mother appearing to you in a dream was anything but fortuitous. The forces of empowerment and disempowerment, which construct a Black woman's reality, are extremely varied, which of course makes it that much more difficult to understand. At the time you were teaching a class on the African American woman and therefore consumed with attempting to understand those aspects of Black female identity formation that proved both functional and dysfunctional. Your mother reminded you of several things. First and most importantly you were not alone; spiritually, she was by your side. Second, she reminded you on a personal level of the effects of Black women's devaluation. As a child and as an adult you saw your mother mentally beaten down because of her Black femaleness and how her mental fatigue framed her whole existence. You said earlier that you were in a quandary about writing this article as well as your purpose in the academy – see, as a Black woman in this society you are constantly having to do battle to prove your worth. You of course know this, but you were only dealing with it on a theoretical and historical level – you thought you could depersonalize by removing yourself and therefore be able to deal with it. But we can never completely remove ourselves and this is what was causing your angst, your questioning of self.

Rochelle: And I should know better, but I thought it would be easier if I could objectively study Black women. I see now (or I remembered) that as Black women we cannot remove ourselves from the study of us. The personal told me that what my mom's life was and what she could not make it become were affected in so many ways, because she did not have the strength to overcome the assaults on her humanity. My Black mother, sisters, aunts, and sister-friends were beautiful and strong and caring and smart and wise and not what society keeps trying to make them out to be. I knew what I needed and began to rethink how to look at and understand jokes that use Black women as the vehicle to laughter.

Once I accepted and begin to work with my anger and disappointment I started to see everything from a much deeper place. It always surprises and saddens me when I experience foolishness from folks who should know better. After the original exchange of yo mama jokes, messages born with wings flew across the listserv, at times slamming my Black female self in the face. The exchanges were angry, sarcastic, and superficial. Although I knew my exasperation with the jokes was justified, it took several days before I was finally able to step back from my original anger and disappointment, so that I might conceptualize the yo mama jokes and their place in the historical devaluation of Black womanhood. I began to realize that within the exchange of views, the animosity cast light on a larger chasm not only between Black men and women, but also between Black people. Our placement within the 'web of reality' was distinctly different and at times oppositional (J. Kincheloe, pers. comm., 16 October 1996). Consequently, disparate views on 'yo mama' become understandable. With this understanding I began to ponder what I believed to be critical questions regarding 'yo mama'.

Once I put my feelings aside long enough to think beyond the anger and disappointment I was able to allow myself to begin to intellectually delve into a historical analysis of the evolution of the dozens which led me to inquire: What does the role of women as the object of assault in the dozens tell us about the place of Black women in the community? How does it reflect and extend the way Black women are shaped by patriarchal power structures? Placing these questions within a Black feminist pedagogical context presented the challenge of how not to dismiss the dozens in their entirety but to reframe their function when analyzed from a critical perspective. As we begin to unearth our subjugated knowledge we are naturally led to ask difficult and sometimes painful questions. I think about my mother and the ways in which a White, patriarchal, racist society thwarted her consciousness. I remember my dream, and my mom's words, 'You've been lied to.' Realizing the lie she spoke of was not about her death but about the misinformation I had been fed my entire life as a Black woman. But the key was to go past the personal and see how the myths and untruths relate to the whole of my existence. The teacher in me needed to ask, how do these various lies undermine the self-concept of African American women, and, importantly, how can this knowledge inform a pedagogy of Black female liberation?

Oshun: I believe you first have to accept or at least understand the conceptual power that is within the jokes. The dozens are powerful weapons because they use 'those aspects of the social order that are unacceptable in any other context, i.e., incest, passive homosexuality, cowardice, taboos and personal defects' (Foster 1986, 216). In opposition to the 'it's only humor' responses that I received via electronic mail, Abrahams states that: 'The art of joking gives a license which permits a restructuring of the world in terms of whatever logic asserts itself' (Abrahams 1972, 229). Jokes are not benign but carry with them nuggets of perceived truth.
Rochelle: Yes, that's what I'm trying to get at. Considered a cultural right by some, the dozens have always been an important aspect of the cultural capital of African American adolescent males. Seen as a 'unique cultural phenomenon' and 'distinctive mode of oppression', the dozens cut across social and class boundaries (Majors and Mancini 1992). For many African Americans, both male and female, the dozens like a cultural heirloom has been passed down from generation to generation. Inasmuch as education seeks to transmit or transfer various copi of information, the dozens represent a major educational legacy in the lives of African Americans. But still I continued to get grief about it all. For some people my basic assumptions concerning the importance of playin' the dozens were simplistic at first glance.
Oshun: Meaning?
Rochelle: I constantly heard that the dozens is a game; it's funny, innocent, and I should stop being such a feminist. I also constantly received the rhetoric regarding the importance of signifying in Black culture. But I see it differently. First, the dozens is a cultural norm that has outlived its usefulness. Second, the dozens has a negative impact on both Black male and female perceptions of Black women.
Oshun: Are they a reflection of or a reaction to?
Rochelle: Good question. I think they are both. Although the dozens are by no means the only way Black females suffer devaluation at the hands of racist, sexist society, I

do believe that they play an important role. I also maintain that a knowledge of the dozens as a cultural phenomenon can serve as a tool in developing a critical pedagogy for African American students. By viewing the dozens through the lens of race, class, and gender and from a Black feminist perspective which acknowledges patriarchy, that which has been viewed as humor or verbal agility can instead be seen as misogynistic and a serious assault on Black women. Accordingly, an analytical dissection of the structures which originally acted as the conduit for the production of the dozens can be used as a basis for an understanding of Black social thought. In order to establish the connection between the dozens and the historic devaluation of Black women it is first necessary to lay a foundation for the study of the dozens. Because I refuse to place myself in one specific camp of thought, I need to use the pieces of various camps that will help me understand and explain the dozens.

The dozens, in some form, originated in West Africa, came to America during enslavement and was transformed and used to help Black men maintain their 'cool' in the face of a cruel and inhumane system. Following enslavement the dozens continued to be played in various sectors of the Black community, eventually becoming canonized which is why (in my opinion) the email argument turned mean at various points. Despite the accepted patriarchal analysis of the benefits of the dozens (a means to manhood, verbal agility, etc.), viewing the game through the lens of Black feminist theory shows its inherent misogyny. Rather than 'business as usual' we deconstruct and search for the whys of the dozens by problematizing our beliefs and assumptions. We ask about its necessity, and we raise questions regarding its affect on Black female devaluation. Importantly we don't run from the answers, even if those answers go against the grain. Ultimately, as an educator we place it all within a pedagogical framework that will engender in our students the ability to read the world and then know what to do with their new awareness.

The theory: Black feminism
Rochelle: Often when research is done on Black women, especially research that examines historical moments in Black women's existence, these women's voices are silenced, or they are portrayed as objects within their own history. It makes sense that I can and should use Black feminist theory in the analysis of the dozens. Black feminist theory understands the nexus of race, class, and gender as controlling forces in Black women's struggles.

Black feminist theory creates the space, as well as the language of critique, that allows us to negotiate between and within theory and knowledge as we search for understanding (Hill-Collins 1991). An understanding of the dozens, their formation, their effects on Black women's image, and the form of resistance Black women enact against negative characterizations has to occur in large part through the use of a theory which articulates the perspective of Black women and acts as a channel for a long denied voice. Negative images of African American women, fabricated in part by the dozens, can best be understood within an ideological framework which produces an understanding of the connection between ideology, stereotypes, and African American women.

Black feminist theory furnishes the space for voice and a self-defined Black woman's standpoint by challenging prevailing approaches to studying oppressed groups (Hill-Collins 1991). The notion exists that the oppressed identify with the powerful and are seen as less human and intellectual and therefore less capable of interpreting or articulating their own oppression. Specifically, Black women's histories have been discussed and analyzed (often incorrectly or at least incompletely and second-hand) by White and Black men, as well as White women who have too often ignored the influence of race, class and gender on the experiences of Black women.

To begin my deconstruction of the dozens I place Black feminist theory in a pedagogy of wholeness, which then allows students to 'read' a popular culture phenomenon through the lens of race, class, and gender (Brock 2005). Students can do a critical analysis from a Black woman's perspective looking at the intersection of race, class, and gender and the historical significance of a Black woman's reality. They are able to deconstruct everyday, seemingly innocent practices and provide an analysis grounded in Black feminist theory.

You know, what really irritates me is that the history of African Americans begins neither in America nor with slavery. When historians or sociologists attempt to produce theories regarding an occurrence in African American culture they either begin their analysis from an ahistorical perspective or insist that all African traits were lost during the centuries of enslavement. Therefore, a casual or causal relationship does not exist. We know that scholarship has substantiated that the slave community maintained and transformed many aspects of African culture – ranging from religion to language to family structure and beyond (Bennett 1988; Herskovits 1958; Raboteau 1978). When I utilize a pedagogy of wholeness or way of knowing, I begin with a historical analysis of the subject under study. For this reason, a scrutiny of the dozens needs to begin with an examination of its occurrence in Africa.

Oshun: Home, sweet home.

Mother-rhyming in Africa

Rochelle: Leading my students to think outside the confines of what they know is always challenging. So much misinformation on Africans and slavery has been fed to us that first we must be on the same page before we deconstruct the present usage of the dozens. I began by contextualizing the connections between Africans in Africa and Africans in the US in an attempt to remove the 'us' and 'them' way of seeing. The lesson is not simply on Africa or on the slave community in the US but a weaving together of the two.

Oshun: I shed an ocean of tears when our homeland was robbed. I remember the majority of my brothers and sisters were taken from West Africa and came primarily from the area drained by the Senegal, Gambia, Volta, Niger, and Congo Rivers (Meier and Rudwick 1976). The African ethnic groups of the Moor, Serere, Taureg, Wolof, Mandingo, Akan, Ewe, Yoruba, Dogan, Ibo, Hausa-Fulani, Angolo, Namib, Ashante, Susu, Baule, Vai, Awikam, Fante, Ga, Seke, Gabon, and Efik became merchandise in the European slave trade and comprised a major part of the African American community (Asante and Mattson 1992). Beginning in Europe, slave ships traveled to Africa where they captured Africans, and sailed to the West Indies where Africans were physically and psychologically broken and trained for enslavement, and then transported to the North and South American mainland. It is among these ethnic groups and ports of the slave trade that we begin our search for the dozens.

Mother-rhyming is the name we used for a dozens-like game back home in West Africa. During my travels, I saw the game played among Ashanti, Gikuku, Yoruba, Efi, Dogan, and some Bantu tribes (Abrahams 1972; Perclay, Monteria, and Dweck 1994). And in the Bantu Wagogo I know that men and boys freely used verbal sexual abuse about grandparents and especially mothers in spoken combat (Rigby 1968). Among the Gusi, close friends exchanged pornographic references about the other's mother and alleged that he would be prepared for incestuous relations with her (Abrahams 1972).

Rochelle: Once we establish the documented use of mother rhyming in specific parts of West Africa we turn to the game elsewhere. I want students to trace the game along the same path used to forcibly bring Africans to US America.

Oshun: The first stop in the slave triangle was the West Indies, which also has a tradition of mother rhyming. Abrahams (1972) has done extensive ethnographic work on the ritualized verbal tradition in several West Indian communities. Plymouth, Tobago, a fishing community, permits mother-rhyming but severely restricts the practice. Abrahams further states that in Nevis, British Leeward Islands the focus of mother-rhyming is on feminine and older people. It's obvious that a version of your dozens has been practiced in West Africa and the West Indies.

Rochelle: Don't call them *my* dozens.

Oshun: As I was saying, mother rhyming and the dozens are in some way kin to one another. Despite what some say, I know that enslaved Africans did not magically forget all that they knew in Africa and that the connection between our African ancestors and African Americans is a strong one. Africans remembered and brought with them to America words and phrases from their native languages that naturally influenced various cultures and behavioral patterns in the 'new' world. The influence of West Africa on African American culture can especially be seen in the West African language of Wolof, which is spoken between the rivers Senegal and Gambia and was the first African language that Europeans came into contact with. Its impact on slave language was considerable since many of the last slaves came from this area. I know that I hear a variety of English words or phrases that illustrate the African influence on African American speech and behavior.

Rochelle: While researching the connections between African and African American culture, I discovered a book by Dalby (1972, 183) called *The African Elements in American English,* where the usage of 'mother' insults in Wolof and Black American English is referenced:

> *mother, yo mama, as a term of severe abuse, or as a term of jocular abuse between friends (incl. use in explicit insults, e.g., mother-fucker). Note similar but less frequent use of father. Cf. use of 'your mother' (less frequently 'your' father) as a term of severe abuse, or as a term of jocular abuse between friends, is in many West African languages, incl. use in explicit insults, literally 'mother-fucker', etc. (esp. in Wolof).

Dalby noted that the impact of Wolof on American English reflects the fact that it is spoken on the stretch of African coastline nearest to the United States. I suspect that forced immigration from this area may have been high at the very end of slavery, since slaveships seeking to make secret runs from Africa to the southern states would have taken the shortest route.

Oshun: Did I ever share with you that I was onboard the Clothilde when it arrived in America in 1859?

Rochelle: No you didn't. But you know what is really interesting is that 1859 was not that long ago, and if we use 30 years as a conservative estimate of the number of years in a generation then the last ship landed a mere four generations ago. And it makes perfect sense to me when African scholars state that 'black Americans [can] look toward a specific area of Africa for a major part of their cultural and linguistic heritage' (Asante and Mattson 1992, 176).

A variation of the dozens was practiced in parts of West Africa. Although in my research I read information on who can joke with whom in various West African tribes, I found little work on how and why they joke. Clearly, it's difficult at this point in my knowledge base to know how widespread the mother-rhyming tradition was in Africa, and how it differs from that in the African American community. What I do know is that joking and mother-rhyming played an important part in the informal verbal traditions in Africa.

African American culture, like African culture, is an oral culture rich with storytelling and verbal repartee (Abrahams 1972). In both cultures the power of words is well respected. Understanding the connection of Africa to African Americans, W.E.B. DuBois was the first person to suggest that the culture of African Americans had been substantially influenced by the cultures of Africa (Meier and Rudwick 1976). Asante and Mattson (1992) state that the first and second generations of Africans in America remember or were told about Africa. These Africans knew the names of rivers, towns, and mountains, and they had at their disposal the rituals, ceremonies, dances, and music of their respective ethnic communities. Although the home they knew was no longer, enslaved Africans used what was remembered from a time in the past to respond to and deal with slavery. I believe it was the physical and psychological dislocation of Africans that served as the impetus in the creation of the dozens.

Oshun: Its creation? What about mother-rhyming in Africa?
Rochelle: Although a form of the dozens was practiced in West Africa it necessarily transformed as the lives of enslaved Africans changed. Life was different in the US than it had been in Africa, so it is logical that although mother-rhyming was practiced, its justification was different in the New World. I mean even the name changed to the dozens.[2]
Oshun: Once your students have analyzed the linguistic and cultural connections between Africa and America, they can begin to critically study the dozens in the slave community. I see how you guide students to contextualize the study and also utilize their critical thinking to draw connections.

The dozens in the new world

Rochelle: I place the study of slavery in its historical context by showing the students the mental and physical scope of enslavement.
Oshun: How?
Rochelle: By giving the students facts. The European slave trade took place between the middle of the fifteenth century and the middle of the nineteenth century and was the largest forced migration in the history of the world. The estimated removal of Africans from their continent ranged between 20 and 50 million (Asante and Mattson 1992). Since complete records of the actual number don't exist, this figure is based on those Africans who actually survived the long, tormenting journey across the middle passage and arrived

in America. The first American slave ship, the Rainbow, set sail in 1645 and as I have already said in 1859 the last slaver, the Clothilde, brought Africans to Mobile, Alabama (Asante and Mattson 1992). Enslavement of Africans lasted close to 400 years and is generally considered one of the cruelest chapters in world history (Bennett 1988).

You were there. Tell me about slave communities.

Oshun: The atrocities committed against enslaved Africans were of the mind, body, and spirit, with the goal of complete acquiescence. As much as possible, I tried to cushion my people from the harshness of their new life, which was no easy task. Systematically deprived of every right of personhood, I saw enslaved Africans struggle to survive in their new home – the plantation. See, the slave community was separate from – while at the same time in response to – the structure of White power and domination, and it was organized into various institutions which provided patterns of behavior for maintaining standards, dealing with the slave master, inducting new members into the group, and expressing the soul and style of the people (Bennett 1988).

Creating a community that could act as a cushion against the assault of a cruel system was as necessary for the slave as with any oppressed people. I see these institutions as paramount for survival on the plantation. If a man, woman, or child, regardless of age or health, committed an infraction of one of the many rules, a severe beating would most likely occur. The most common offense was impudence which according to Fredrick Douglass:

> might mean almost anything, or nothing at all, just according to the caprice of the master or overseer at the moment. But, whatever it is, or is not, if it gets the name 'impudence,' the party charged with it is sure of a flogging. This offense may be committed in various ways; in the tone of an answer; in answering at all; in not answering; in the expression of the countenance; in the motion of the head; in the gait, manner and bearing of the slave. (quoted in Bennett 1988, 94)

We had to be 'crafty' in order to survive. Expressing any form of emotion was paramount to punishment, so slaves mastered the skill of removing themselves mentally from a situation, becoming adept at developing methods by which they could mask their true feelings. Rather playing the buffoon, the happy-singing slave, pretending ignorance of the infraction, using simple utterances in response to a command, or a host of other survival techniques, enslaved Africans developed various modes of survival. For male slaves the dozens was one of these forms.

Rochelle: For my students, I continuously draw the connections between Africans in West Africa and Africans/African Americans in the United States. For instance, we know that a form of mother-rhyming existed in various West African tribes and these tribes, especially Wolof, were the direct ancestors of the slave community. Slaves were sold between plantations that existed in various locales, and therefore the slave culture did not remain in an enclave.

A transformed version of the mother-rhyming that was prevalent in West African cultures became part of the new slave community. For Africans in the New World, mother-rhyming became a 'song of survival', which offset the pain of not being able to express their true feelings in front of their masters (Perclay, Monteria, and Dweck 1994). In her autobiography Ossie Guffy (1971, 48) recalls her grandfather describing the dozens:

> When I was coming up I heard about that game, only I heard about it the way it used to be, and I heard how it started and why it started. It was a game slaves used to play, only they wasn't just playing for fun. They was playing to teach themselves and their sons how to stay alive. The whole idea was to learn to take whatever the master said to you without answering back or hitting him, 'cause that was the way the slave had to be so he could go on living.

Rochelle: The game afforded a skill that allowed male slaves to endure an unendurable system. Can you imagine the necessity of such a game for male slaves in that it taught them how to maintain and control their anger and frustration?

Oshun: Question. If the dozens were the vehicle to teach male slaves endurance, what did the female slaves use? I mean, enslavement was just as harsh on them so what did they do?

Rochelle: Good question. This becomes a perfect time to allow my students to creatively imagine what strategies female slaves developed. I ask students to take this part of the discussion in two opposite directions. First they brainstorm possible strategies and I let them be as *out there* with those strategies as they want. The second step is to see which of their brainstormed strategies they can tie into the various class readings. In both cases I always get some pretty interesting strategies and an extremely rich discussion.

The dozens and African American women

> Nealee started out but she couldn't or wouldn't make it. She was being driven to the west African coast for sale when she became ill and refused to walk another step. Mungo Park, who was one of the last persons to see Nealee, said she was put on an ass but the ass was so very unruly, that no sort of treatment could induce him to proceed with his load and as Nealee made no exertion to prevent herself from falling, she was quickly thrown off, and had one of her legs much bruised. Every attempt to carry her forward being thus found ineffectual, the general cry of the coffel [slave caravan] was, kang-tegi, kang-tegi, 'cut her throat, cut her throat' an operation I did not wish to see performed, and therefore marched onwards with the foremost of the coffel. I had not walked above a mile when one of Kara's [the leader] domestic slaves came to me, with poor Nealee's garment upon the end of his bow and exclaimed, 'Nealee affeeleeta' (Nealee is lost). I asked him whether the Slattees had given him the garment as a reward for cutting her throat, he replied that Kara and the schoolmaster would not consent to that measure, but had left her on there at where undoubtedly she soon perished, and was probably devoured by wild beast. (Bennett 1988, 30)

Oshun: I remember. I held Nealee close to me as she took her last breath and was set free.

Rochelle: Perhaps Nealee knew what was in store for her as an African woman in US America. On some level while walking in that coffel she pictured the sexual abuse she would receive as the property of an inhumane society. Maybe she saw the battle her granddaughters and great-granddaughters would have to wage as African American women just to receive the rights and privileges shown to White women. Could it be that she foresaw Zora Neale Hurston (1978, 29) writing 300 years later that the, 'Nigger woman is de mule of de world', and therefore refused to ride that mule into bondage? Nealee must have known the system of degradation that was imminent, inasmuch as it eventually came to pass for African women in America. Oh yes, even a brother from the macho 60s wrote that: 'It has been the Negro woman, more than anyone else, who has borne the constant agonies of racial barbarity in America, from the very first day she was bought in chains to this soil' (Hernton 1965, 10).

The sexual offenses against slave women by White men have been well documented (Giddings [1992]1995; Hill-Collins 1991; hooks 1993). There existed an economic necessity for slavery and therefore the proliferation of slaves. The fact that slave women were used for breeding is well known, as is the knowledge that sexual relations, whether voluntary or involuntary, occurred between slave women and their masters. In fact another theory on the origins of the name dozens states that the term may have in fact been meant to represent the (opponent's) mother as being one of the dozens of women available to the sexual whims of her master (Majors and Mancini 1992; Perclay, Monteria, and Dweck 1994).

Remember the need to question the world as we discussed earlier? Well here is where it becomes extremely important for students. They have to question women's place in the dozens and if they stop at the first question then they feel the 'Wrath of Rochelle'. Were women used because of their sacred place in the community (Foster 1986; Grier and Price 1968, 1971; Perclay, Monteria, and Dweck 1994) or because of a more intricately woven connection between the abuse slave women suffered and the resulting pathology these abuses developed in men? Although it has been asserted by many historians that the slave system in the US serves as a useful trajectory to describe the particular form of oppression that African American women experienced (Giddings [1992]1995; Hill-Collins 1991; hooks 1993; Jordan 1992), scholars writing about the dozens have not connected its usage of women as objects of insults with this devaluation. Instead, the dozens have mainly been viewed from a patriarchal framework.

For example, Majors and Mancini (1992) state that young males are often brought closer to the needs and feelings of their mothers because of their father's absence and inability to provide for the family. Because African American boys are constantly exposed to the problems and sacrifices of their mother's attempt to raise a family, they may become unexpectedly sensitive, protective, and empathetic toward their mother and other women. Based on this sense of protection, mothers and women are used in the dozens as the ultimate hurtful insult. In this same vein, Foster believes that the dozens requires Black boys to put aside a mother's special sanctification. According to Foster (1986, 219), 'The natural inclination to defend a mother's honor must be suppressed as young black males move to their world of men where love of a mother is perverted in the medium of wit.' Clearly, according to the aforementioned authors, Black women are objectified, vilified, and dehumanized in a man's attempt at independence. Ain't that some shit?

Oshun: Okay we have discussed and attempted to outline a theoretical framework for the study of the dozens in the African American community. So how do you frame the conversation with your students? How do you explain what makes the dozens of enslavement different than or distinct from the dozens of today?

Rochelle: As a class we analyze several things. An important question in understanding the affective consequences of the dozens is an in-depth analysis of the contextual ideology of society as the game has been historically practiced. How has the ideology undergirding the dozens changed? Within this analysis we can begin to understand the spirit of the game as it relates to the continued devaluation of Black women. Of course ideology not only supports but also constructs our views, beliefs, feelings and opinions on lived reality. Consequently, Asante and Atwater state that, '[H]ierchal discourse which seeks to maintain its hierchal position is supported by ideology. Without the ideological context, the discourse is vacuous, empty, a hollow form without power' (1986, 170). Through ideology the social justification underlying jokes remains hidden, or at the very least mystified. Klump and Hollihan observed:

> Ritual is not only the essential process of reaffirming a piety, but also the process of a rebirth through which ideology may be changed. Whether an event precipitates a conservative ritual reaffirming an old ideology or a new ideology depends on the rhetoric surrounding it. (quoted in Gresson 1995, 175)

I struggle to get my students to understand that the hegemonic nature of humor allows racist, patriarchal, misogynist jokes to be viewed as an innocuous, funny bit of non-factual information, never allowing for the space to exist for a form of feminist critique. Instead, we are forewarned to believe only that the dozens have always been a cultural necessity aimed at initiating Black men into a racist society. Gresson (1995, 176) maintains that a critical form of collusion operates in racist joking and by extension patriarchal misogynist jokes in the form of the dozens: 'The shared stance that no continuity exists between the public and personal domains ... is precisely this shared stance of nonrelationship that sustains both objective (public) and subjective (private) actions of racism.'

Oshun: That all sounds smart and necessary, but what do you really mean?
Rochelle: We play detective and seek answers to unknown questions. The class analyzes every aspect of joking – the how and why of the jokes. We ask what makes the jokes hurtful to others. Why is the sexuality of women used as a means of insult instead of that of men? We look at how the jokes might have been used in West Africa,[3] how we know they were reported to have been used during slavery and how they are used today and then we layer in the historical realities of the women during those various times and places.

Next we place our epistemological assumptions into a Black feminist frame of reference. It's important that we discuss and understand the application of a study of the dozens to a pedagogy of liberation and empowerment of Black females. To be empowered is to recreate the definition of the *other*, and redefining the other is a goal of a Black feminist epistemology. This definition is one that comes from Black women themselves, instead of being placed on them. Black feminist epistemology offers two significant contributions toward understanding self and designing a pedagogy of empowerment. First, a Black feminist epistemology fosters a fundamental paradigmatic shift in how we think about oppression. By embracing a paradigm of race, class, and gender as interlocking systems of oppression, a Black feminist epistemology reconceptualizes the social relations of domination and resistance. Second, a Black feminist epistemology addresses ways of assessing 'truth' and reality of Black women. Empowerment is manifested in the individual when they are able to define their reality and name their truth.

Oshun: Do they 'get it'? I mean your students.
Rochelle: Sometimes they do. Even though they may call me 'the angry Black woman', they understand the various levels of the all-consuming nature of negativity that surrounds Black women. The knowledge that an Afriwomanist epistemology engenders allows us to understand the effects of controlling images of Black women (hooks 1993). Once gained, students view everything in their world with an eye of critique – jokes, videos, movies, television, etc. They begin to see the pervasive nature of the negative images of Black women in movies, in magazines, on television, on

billboards, on the news and in the paper and understand how some Black women acquiesce to those images, believing them real.

Instead our dominant knowledge of self provides us with the needed strength and wisdom to get rid of and subvert the stereotypes and controlling images, causing them to lose their control to define. I also make sure they understand this is no easy task. Remember my own angst at being silenced that led to my dream? We can all fall victim to the place society attempts to put us, so it is all that more important to find ways out.

Oshun: Yes and redefining our knowledge begets empowerment, which forces a reconceptualization of the power relations that control and define our society. African American women have been victimized by race, gender, and class oppression, but portraying Black women as passive, unfortunate recipients of racial and sexual abuse denies the legacy of resistance and struggle which has always been a part of Black women's lives. Similarly, presenting African American women solely as heroic figures who easily engage in resisting oppression on all fronts minimizes the very real cost of oppression and can foster the perception that Black women need no help because we can 'take it'.

When I tell students that it was a Black woman that initially sent the jokes on the listserv they begin to see how ideology can *blind* us to seeing how we can become part of our own oppression. We must develop a true grounded history of the role of Black women in America. Accept and be proud of the truth but also accept what we have done and are doing that hurts us!

Rochelle: Understanding how a Black feminist consciousness leads to activism and the determination to fight for social justice is important for especially students to understand. The dynamics between consciousness and activism have the goal that the world is not someplace where we must be tolerated or that we want or have to find some quiet corner and hide away. Instead, we look at the world as something, given the right tools, we can change. With agency we gain the ability to act on and change our world/environment, always remembering that while we want and strive for individual empowerment, only collective action can effectively generate lasting social transformation of political and economic institutions. This knowledge gives students the responsibility to 'do something', become an agent for change. I constantly tell my students that with knowledge comes responsibility to change the world. Important to a pedagogy of wholeness and which I have not discussed yet is the social justice aspect. The new way of reading the world is not frivolous – we learn new ways of thinking and seeing so that we can make the changes in our society that need to be made – so that we can address the problems that need to be addressed.

The deconstruction of the ideologies undergirding the dozens affords a new paradigm and a Black woman's pedagogy. Once controlling images are understood by students, they can begin to see these images in music videos, television commercials, advertisements and importantly a ritualized verbal game of insults, which make obvious and overt references 'to alleged or incestuous activities of the opponent's mother, grandmother, daughters, sisters, wife, or other female relatives' (Foster 1986, 215). We can proclaim to the spirit of Nealee, and all the Black women since that within us lies the power to resist and change that which does not make us stronger.

Oshun: You go girl!

Notes

1. The most common names I found in my research that are also the most fitting, are the dozens and mother rhyming (Foster 1986). For purposes of distinction, mother-rhyming will be used when referring to the 'game' in West Africa and the West Indies. The term 'dozens' will be used when referring to the game in the African American community.
2. One theory on the genesis of the name states that the term 'dozens' originated in slavery where after the middle passage, scurvy ravaged many of the slaves and the 12 most 'damaged' Africans were sold at a bargain rate – the dirty dozen. Supposedly, the only thing more degrading than slavery was to be part of the dirty dozen and degrading a person's mother was to make them 'feel as low as one of the dirty dozen' (Perclay, Monteria, and Dweck 1994, 8).
3. In answering this question I ask my students to utilize Bartlett's (1928) constructed imagination since short of a time machine and without specific primary source research we must instead each use the information at hand and then 'wonder'.

References

Abrahams, R.D. 1972. Joking: The training of the man of words in talking broad. In *Rappin' and stylin' out: Communication in urban Black America*, ed. T. Kochman, 215–41. Urbana, IL: University of Illinois Press.

Asante, M.K., and D. Atwater. 1986. The rhetorical condition as symbolic structure in discourse. *Communication Quarterly* 34, no. 2: 170–7.

Asante, M.K., and M.T. Mattson. 1992. *Historical and cultural atlas of African Americans*. New York: Macmillan.

Bartlett, F.E. 1928. Types of imagination. *Journal of Philosophical Studies* 3: 78–85.

Bennett, L., Jr. 1988. *Before the Mayflower: A history of Black America*. 6th ed. New York: Penguin Books.

Brock, R. 1999. Theorizing away the pain: Hyphenating the space between the personal and the pedagogical. Unpublished doctoral diss., Pennsylvania State University.

Brock, R. 2005. *Sista talk: The personal and the pedagogical.* New York: Peter Lang.

Cavanagh, S. 2005. Lawmakers ratchet up graduation requirements. *Education Week* 25, no. 2: 30.

Dalby, D. 1972. The African element in American English. In *Rappin' and stylin' out: Communication in urban Black America*, ed. T. Kochman, 170–88. Urbana, IL: University of Illinois Press.

Denzin, N.K. 1998. The art and politics of interpretation. In *Collecting and interpreting qualitative materials*, ed. N.K. Denzin and Y.S. Lincoln, 313–44. Thousand Oaks, CA: Sage.

Denzin, N.K., and Y.S. Lincoln. 1998. Entering the field of qualitative research. In *Strategies of qualitative inquiry*, ed. N.K. Denzin and Y.S. Lincoln, 1–34. Thousand Oaks, CA: Sage.

Fine, M. 1998. Working in the hyphens: Reinventing self and other in qualitative research. In *The landscape of qualitative research*, ed. N.K. Denzin and Y.S. Lincoln, 130–55. Thousand Oaks, CA: Sage.

Foster, H.L. 1986. *Ribbin', jivin', and playin' the dozens: The persistent dilemma in our schools.* Boston, MA: Ballinger.

Giddings, P. [1992]1995. The last taboo. In *Words of fire: An anthology of African American feminist thought*, ed. B. Guy-Sheftall, 414–28. New York: The New York Press.

Gresson, A.D. 1995. *The recovery of race in America.* Minneapolis, MN: University of Minnesota Press.

Grier, W.H., and M.C. Price. 1968. *Black rage.* New York: Basic Books.

Grier, W.H., and M.C. Price. 1971. *The Jesus bag.* New York: McGraw-Hill.

Guffy, O. 1971. *The autobiography of a Black woman by Ossie Guffy as told to Gerda Lerner.* 1st ed. New York: Norton.

Hernton, C.C. 1965. *Sex and racism in America.* New York: Grove Press.

Herskovits, M. 1958. *The myth of the Negro past.* Boston, MA: Beacon Press.

Hill-Collins, P. 1991. *Black feminist thought: Knowledge, consciousness and the politics of empowerment.* New York: Routledge.

hooks, b. 1993. *Sisters of the yam: Black women and self-recovery.* Boston, MA: South End Press.

Hurston, Z.N. 1978. *Their eyes were watching God.* Urbana, IL: University of Illinois Press.

Jordan, J. 1992. *Technical difficulties: African-American notes on the state of the union.* New York: Pantheon Books.

Kincheloe, J. 2005. Describing the bricolage: Conceptualizing a new rigor in qualitative research. *Qualitative Inquiry* 11, no. 3: 323–50.

Majors, R., and J.B. Mancini. 1992. *Cool pose: The dilemmas of black manhood in America.* New York: Lexington Books.

Meier, A., and E. Rudwick. 1976. *From plantation to ghetto.* 3rd ed. New York: Hill & Wang.

Perclay, J., I. Monteria, and S. Dweck. 1994. *Snaps: If ugliness were bricks your mother would be a housing project ... and more than 450 other snaps, caps, and insults for playing the dozens.* New York: Quill William Morrow.

Raboteau, A.J. 1978. *Slave religion: The 'invisible institution' in the antebellum south.* Oxford/London: Oxford University Press.

Richardson, L. 1998. Writing: A method of inquiry. In *Collecting and interpreting qualitative materials*, ed. N.K. Denzin and Y.S. Lincoln, 345–71. Thousand Oaks, CA: Sage.

Rigby, P. 1968. Joking relationships, kin categories and clanship among the Gogo. *Africa* 38, no. 2: 133–54.

Sternberg, B.J. 2006. Real improvement for real students: Test smarter, serve better. *Harvard Educational Review* 76, no. 4: 557–63.

Index

Page numbers followed by 'n' refer to notes

Abrahams, R.D. 125, 128
academy: and REDO process 20–2
achievement: and intelligence 76–7
Adams, M.: Bell, L.A.; and Griffin, P. 38
Admongo 51
advertising: branding 51–2; schoolroom images 51–5
Adweek magazine 51
African American women 131–4
African Elements in American English, The (Dalby) 128
African mother-rhyming: and Dozens game 127–9, 130
Ali-Khan, C. 43–62
Appadurai, A. 58
Apple, M. 8, 50
Asante, M.K.: and Atwater, D. 132–3; and Mattson, D.K. 129

Bakhtin, M. 91, 107
Banks, J. 27, 28
Bartlett, F.E. 122
Basu, J.S.: and Barton, A. 39
Bell, L.A.: Adams, M.; and Griffin, P. 38
Berger, J. 56
black feminist theory 119–36; Dozens game 121–3; empowerment 124
Bohman, J. 28
Bourdieu, P. 54
branding: and advertising 51–2
Brock, R. 119–36
Brown, T.: and DeGennaro, D. 58

Carter, R. 57
Cartwright, L.: and Sturken, M. 45
Casper, M.J.: and Moore, L.J. 49
Chaplin, E. 58
childhood: absent images 49–50; advertising schoolroom images 51–5; schoolchildren images 48–9; and visual information 45–6; and worldly kids 46–8
citizenship 67; civil 28, 29–30, 33, 36, 37, 38; concept 27; and full participation 28, 37; political 28, 30–1, 36; social 28, 31, 33, 36; social justice and urban science education 25–41; and students' expression 37–8; and 3Cs model 36;
civil citizenship 28, 29–30, 33, 36, 37, 38
class: demography 68n; instructions 69–71; neighbourhood 64–7
classism: photo essays and oppression 70, 72, 73, 76, 77, 79, 80
classroom: collaboration 83–101; contact zones 106–7; layout and ethnic distribution 34; material resources 34–5
Cloud, C. 55
co-researching 83, 95
co-teaching 84, 86, 87, 88, 91, 95; political citizenship and urban science education 30–1, 36
co-writing 86, 95
cogenerative dialogues 83, 85, 86, 87, 88, 89, 91; civil citizenship and urban science education 29–30, 33, 36, 37, 38
collaboration: classrooms 83–101; co-researching 83, 95; co-teaching 84, 86, 87, 88, 91, 95; co-writing 86, 95; cogenerative dialogues 83, 85, 86, 87, 88, 89, 91; collective endeavour 89–91; complexities 85–6; field-based science methods course 83–101; multi-logicality 94; other-awareness 92; phenomenological and individual experience 91–3; roles and hierarchies 95–6; teacher role reconstruction 93–4, 98
collective endeavour 89–91
colonialism 10
constructive imagination 122
contact zones: classroom 106–7
Coontz, S. 46
cosmopolitanism: social citizenship and urban science education 31, 33
counter storytelling 64, 80
critical epistemology: and visual knowledge 43–62

INDEX

critical pedagogy: existential and political 2; personal and practical 2–3
critical praxis *see* teacher educators and critical praxis
critical research: knowledge hierarchies 7–23

Dalby, D. 128
Debord, G. 54
DeGennaro, D.: and Brown, T. 58
Denzin, N.K.: and Lincoln, Y.S. 120; Lincoln, Y.S.; and Guardina, M.D. 10
dialogues *see* cogenerative dialogues
Douglass, F. 130
Dozens game: African American women 131–4; African mother-rhyming 127–9, 130; black feminist theory 121–36; conceptual power 125; cultural phenomenon 125–6; enslavement 126, 127, 129–30; new world 129–31; origins 126; West Africa 129, 130; West Indies 128
DuBois, W.E.B. 129
Durham, M.G.: and Kellner, D. 54, 57
Dyer, R. 50

Eastwood, C. 66–7
Ellsworth, E. 112
Elmesky, R.: and Tobin, K. 39
Emdin, C. 25–41
empowerment: black feminist theory 124
endeavour: collective 89–91
English, L.: and Lander, D. 86, 91
enslavement: Dozens game 126, 127, 129–30
epistemology: critical and visual knowledge 43–62
ethnic distribution: and classroom layout 34
experience: phenomenological and individual 91–3
expression: students and citizenship 37–8

feeling 75–6
feminist theory: black 119–36
Fendler, L. 105, 110
Flags of Our Fathers 66–7
Foster, H.L. 132
Fram, S.: and Margolis, E. 47, 55, 58
Freire, P. 1, 2, 11, 48, 104, 105, 112; and Shor, I. 97

Giroux, H. 44, 50, 55
Greene, M. 85
Gresson, A.D. 133
Griffin, P.: Adams, M.; and Bell, L.A. 38
Guardina, M.D.: Denzin, N.K.; and Lincoln, Y.S. 10
Guffy, O. 130–1

hermeneutic phenomenology 87

hermeneutics: of vulnerability 114
hierarchies: knowledge 7–23, 96; and roles 95–6
Higonnet, A. 45, 46
Hill-Collins, P. 123
Hollihan, T.A.: and Klumpp, J.F. 133
Home Alone 46
Hurtson, Z.N. 131

images: absent childhood 49–50; creation and visual knowledge 57–8; reading 55; schoolchildren 48–50; schoolroom 51–5
imagination: constructive 122
individual and phenomenological experience 91–3
information: visual 45–6
intelligence: and achievement 76–7

journals: reflective teaching 110–12, 117
justice: social 7, 25–41

Kealy, W. 57
Kellner, D.: and Durham, M.G. 54, 57
Kenny, K. 44, 57
kids *see* childhood
Kincheloe, J.L. 11, 20, 44, 46, 50–1, 53–5, 93; and Steinberg, S.R. 49; and Tobin, K. 10
Klumpp, J.F.: and Hollihan, T.A. 133
knowledge: burden 7–8, 9, *see also* visual knowledge
knowledge hierarchies 7–23, 96; dismantle 13, 19; examine 13, 17–19; open 13, 20; REDO (Reveal/Examine/Dismantle/Open) process 12–22; reveal 12–13, 17; stepping out 10–12
Kress, T.M. 1–6, 7–23, 57, 58, 96
Kundera, M. 43

Lander, D.: and English, L. 86, 91
Law, J. 69
Lee, S. 66–7
Lesko, N. 50
Letters from Iwo Jima 66–7
Lincoln, Y.S.: and Denzin, N.K. 120; Denzin, N.K.; and Guardina, M.D. 10
Lipman, P. 27
literacy: visual 55–8
Lorde, A. 11, 12

Majors, R.: and Mancini Billson, J. 132
Margolis, E.: and Fram, S. 47, 55, 58
Marshall, T.H. 28
Mattson, D.K.: and Asante, M.K. 129
metalogue 96
Miller, T. 49
Mirzoeff, N. 58
Moore, L.J.: and Casper, M.J. 49
mother-rhyming: African 127–9, 130

INDEX

multi-logicality 94
MySpace 57

No Child Left Behind (NCLB) 103–4

official knowledge 8
oppression: photo essays 63–82
Oshun 122–34
other-awareness 92
others: seeing 55–6

participation: full and citizenship 28, 37
Paugh, P.: and Robinson, E. 103–18
pedagogy: critical 2–3
Pedersen, C. 58
phenomenological and individual experience 91–3
phenomenology: hermeneutic 87
photo essays and oppression 63–82; class demography 68n; class instructions 69–71; class neighbourhood 64–7; classism 70, 72, 73, 76, 77, 79, 80; feeling 75–6; intelligence and achievement 76–7; literal theme interpretation 72–4, 77; metaphorical theme interpretation 74–5; racism 70, 72, 74, 75, 79, 80; sexism 70, 72, 73, 76, 79, 80; study methods and procedures 67–9; unsettled expertise theme 76–9
play: reflective 110–12
Pocohontas 66
political citizenship 28, 30–1, 36
positivism 10
power: conceptual 125; dynamics 112
Pratt, M.L. 106
praxis: critical *see* teacher educators and critical praxis
PT Quigley 52

racism 70, 72, 74, 75, 79, 80
Reading First Initiative 103
reading images 55
REDO (Reveal/Examine/Dismantle/Open) process: and the academy 20–2; and knowledge hierarchies 9, 12–22
reflection: tool 110
reflective play 110–12
reflective teaching journals 110–12, 117
rhetoric: visual 44
Robinson, E.: and Paugh, P. 103–18
roles: and hierarchies 95–6; teacher 93–4, 98
Rose, G. 45, 58
Roth, W-M.: and Tobin, K. 7

schoolchildren: images and visual knowledge 48–50
schoolroom images 51–5
schools: and visual literacy 55–8

Schutz, A. 92
science 38–9; field-based methods course 83–101, *see also* urban science education
seeing others 55–6
Sensoy, O. 50, 56, 63–82
Sewell, W.H. 7
sexism 70, 72, 73, 76, 79, 80
Shor, I.: and Freire, P. 97
Siry, C.A.: and Zawatski, E. 83–101
Smith, L.T. 10
social citizenship 28, 31, 33, 36
social justice 67; and 3Cs model 36; citizenship and urban science education 25–41; and classroom material resources 34–5; science 38–9
Solórzano, D.G.: and Yosso, T.J. 64
standardization: and system challenges 114–16
Steinberg, S.R.: and Kincheloe, J.L. 49
storytelling: counter 64, 80
students: expression and citizenship 37–8
Sturken, M.: and Cartwright, L. 45
Sue, D.W.: *et al* 25
system challenges: and standardization 114–16

Tavin, K. 59
teacher: education 85; role reconstruction 93–4, 98
teacher educators and critical praxis 103–18; contact zones 106–7; critical stance adoption 104–6; generative words 105, 112; hermeneutics of vulnerability 114; power dynamics 112; reflection tool 110; reflective play 110–12; reflective teaching journals 110–12, 117; standardization and system challenges 114–16; vigilant critique 105, 110
teaching: reflective journals 110–12, 117, *see also* co-teaching
3Cs model: and citizenship 36; and urban science education 28–9
Tiananmen Square (China) 68–9
Time magazine 46, 47, 56
Tobin, K. 58; and Elmesky, R. 39; and Kincheloe, J.L. 10; and Roth, W-M. 7

unsettled expertise theme 76–9
urban science education: citizenship and social justice 25–41; classroom layout and ethnic distribution 34; cogenerative dialogues and civil citizenship 29–30, 33, 36, 37, 38; cosmopolitanism and social citizenship 31, 36; co-teaching and political citizenship 30–1, 36; data analysis 33; data collection 32–3; social justice research design 32; and three Cs 28–9

INDEX

vigilant critique 105, 110
visual information: and children 45–6
visual knowledge: advertising schoolroom images 51–5; childhood and visual information 45–6; childhood and worldliness 46–8; and critical epistemology 43–62; and image creation 57–8; schoolchildren images 48–9; spectacle and capital 54–5; under-represented childhood images 49–50; visual literacy and schools 55–8
visual literacy 55–8; and reading images 55; and seeing others 55–6
visual rhetoric 44
visuality 45
vulnerability: hermeneutics 114

Way We Never Were, The (Coontz) 46
Wenders, W. 55
West Africa: Dozens game 129, 130
West Indies: Dozens game 128
Widener, J. 68–9
women: African American 131–4; African mother 127–9, 130
worldly kids 46–8
writing 86, 95

Yosso, T.J.: and Solórzano, D.G. 64

Zawatski, E.: and Siry, C.A. 83–101